RISE

an anthology of Power and Unity

Introduction by Eugene B. Redmond
Selection/Edition by Mark Lipman

Vagabond
Venice, California

FAIR USE NOTICE

VAGABOND asserts, under Section 107 of the Copyright Act, the right to use the artwork herein to illustrate this anthology, RISE (an anthology of Power and Unity), done so for purposes of education and that the nature of the material used relates to copyright's purpose of encouraging creative expression.

Edition Copyright © 2017 by Mark Lipman, editor
Front cover art based on *Rising Tide*, unknown artist; and
The Hand That Will Rule the World – One Big Union, by Ralph "Bingo" Chaplin.
Back cover art based on the *Detroit Industry Mural*, by Diego Rivera.
All rights reserved.

No part of this book may be reproduced by any means,
including, information storage and retrieval or photocopying
except for short excerpts quoted in critical articles,
without the written permission of the publisher.

editor@vagabondbooks.net

Published by VAGABOND
Mark Lipman, editor

VAGABOND Collection

Intellectual Property
reverts back to the individual poet / artist upon publication.
RISE (AN ANTHOLOGY OF POWER AND UNITY)
1st ed. / p.cm.

ISBN 13: 978-1-936293-28-5

Made in the USA

"Be formless, shapeless, like water.... Be water, my friend."
~ Bruce Lee

Table of Contents

10 ~ *Forward by Mark Lipman*
12 ~ *Introduction by Eugene B. Redmond*

Ángel L. Martínez
15 ~ Every Day is An Ancestor's Day
16 ~ Slavery Behind Counters
 and Behind Bars

Adam Gottlieb
17 ~ Revolution Blues
19 ~ Here's to the Road

Dorothy "Dottie" Payne
21 ~ No Song Can Be Sung

Eric Allen Yankee
26 ~ America
28 ~ The Day America Died

Adrian Ernesto Cepeda
30 ~ 17 Years, 16 Shots

Dee Allen
31 ~ How Many More?
32 ~ Rebel X

Eleanor Goldfield
34 ~ Dear White Privilege

Irene Monica Sanchez
38 ~ We are Rising

Anmarie Soucie
42 ~ American Spring

Anika Paris
44 ~ Iron Claw
45 ~ Bullets in the Sky

M. A. Peterson
47 ~ The American Machine
51 ~ The Over-Employed

Henry Howard
53 ~ Women on Fire

Carlos Raúl Dufflar
57 ~ We Are All Jimmy Baldwin
60 ~ Asere Bill Epton

Jackie Lopez
62 ~ I Come from Trash
64 ~ Love is Stronger than Hate:
 Poem for the Ages

Elizabeth Marino
67 ~ Litany for Peace

Alessandra Bava
68 ~ Abuse of Power

Tim Hall
69 ~ And I Say Power to the People
71 ~ Autumn Leaves

Victor Avila
73 ~ The Black Handkerchief
 (Ayotinapa)

Juan Cárdenas
75 ~ Cortez Continues

Chris Devcich
76 ~ Social Justice
78 ~ We Got Cops Killing
     Kids of Color Constantly

Teresa Mei Chuc
81 ~ Breath

Michael Castro
82 ~ Double Kwansaba after Michael Brown
83 ~ Report from the Streets
     around St. Louis

Karen Melander-Magoon
87 ~ Sandtown, Home of Freddie Gray
88 ~ Shadow

Iris De Anda
91 ~ Say Her Name
93 ~ Some Say

Antonieta Villamil
94 ~ Brutality Games
95 ~ Song for the Worker Woman

S.L. Kerns
96 ~ An Amendment in Angst
97 ~ Gun at My Head

Gabor Gyukics
98 ~ Guardian Angels?

Lynn White
99 ~ Thoughts on Swallowing a Butterfly

Luis J. Rodriguez
101 ~ Poem for a New Dream

Dawnna "Ashay" Mathieu
106 ~ Slaves No More

Sherman Pearl
109 ~ Hands of the Convict

Paul David Adkins
110 ~ Edward Menefee, Murdered Inmate,
Attica Prison Rebellion, September 13th, 1971
111 ~ Alfred Williams, Murdered Inmate,
Attica Prison Rebellion, September 13th, 1971

Megan D. Robinson
113 ~ Authority Revisioned

Joshua Hegarty
115 ~ Black & Blue
116 ~ Elegy

Jeffery Martin
117 ~ No Consequences

Jessica M. Wilson Cárdenas
120 ~ Epitaph: In this History

Arthur Hurts
122 ~ Not Afraid to Speak the Truth
123 ~ The Blood-Splattered Banner

Ernest Rosenthal
124 ~ Mockit

Peter Coco
126 ~ Wall Mart

Patrick A. Harford
128 ~ A Short Poem
128 ~ Mining Meaning

David A. Romero
129 ~ Company Store

R. Bremner
132 ~ My Landlord Otto
      (or, the 102 Main Avenue Blues)

Gloria Vando
133 ~ Karma

Camari Carter
135 ~ What is It Like to be Black?
138 ~ The New Black

Diamanda Galás
141 ~ Song from the Blood
      of Those Murdered

Fred Dodsworth
143 ~ Orange Ain't the New Black

David S. Pointer
148 ~ Calling Car 2016

El Williams III
149 ~ Black Magic

Dylan Garcia
150 ~ Homegrown

John Kaniecki
153 ~ Cycles of Murder in Fort Hood
157 ~ The Worker Shall Rise

Tim Kahl
159 ~ Ode to a Tomato Truck
160 ~ After the Wheatland Hop Riot

Ayo Ayoola-Amale
161 ~ An Untold Fire is Dead
162 ~ The Dawn of My Being

Michael Schiffman
163 ~ Do They Know Who They Are?
164 ~ The Sewing Floor

Christian Elder
167 ~ #aninsignificantman
170 ~ People of No Color

Jack Hirschman
173 ~ The Street Vote Arcane
175 ~ The Miwok Arcane

Maria Elena Danelli
177 ~ Someone Said the Sun Had Died

Nina Serrano
178 ~ Lolita Lebron

Isaac J Torres
184 ~ Rosetta's Stone

Mahnaz Badihian
186 ~ The World Over

Stan Ginsburg
187 ~ The Embarcadero is a Place
      Where Lawyers Live

Lawrence Ferlinghetti
191 ~ The First and the Last
      of Everything
193 ~ The Last Lord's Prayer

Eugene B. Redmond
195 ~ Wakin' & *Walkin'*:
      The Mournin' After
196 ~ An Epistolary Journal

Mark Lipman
199 ~ for the Deeds of Men Live on
202 ~ Amiri Baraka

205 ~ **Index of Artwork**

FORWARD

In Times Like These

> *"May you live in interesting times."*
> *~ an alleged Chinese curse*

This morning, America has finally awoken from its dream to find itself standing upon the precipice, the very edge of oblivion, with one foot hanging over the cliff into the abyss. There's a shudder, a scream and then silence.

These are the times in which we live, a time of crisis, ripe with both danger and opportunity. Where we go from here, the destiny of us all, now depends on the choices we make today. Will we cower and hide our heads, hoping to make do and get through, while the final bolts are set into place, or will we, as a people, with courage in our hearts and sweat on our brows, with an aching for justice in the very fiber of our bones rise up and say, "Enough!"?

In times such as these the decisions we make will have repercussions throughout history, shaping the lives of future generations to come and the fate of this very planet. The situation is that dire, and as members of the human race – we are all responsible.

As human beings, it is our duty to resist tyranny and oppression – especially when we ourselves are not the targets of that injustice. Either we stand together or we fall apart. For by remaining silent, "When they came for me, there was no one left to speak up." ❖

In times like these we must show what we are made of.

It is not a question of one person doing everything, but of everyone doing ... and doing what they can. That is the whole meaning of *Together*.

As poets, writers, artists and free-thinkers, having often faced the realities and brutalities of an unjust system first-hand, where the disparity of wealth has created the richest country in the world that leads the world in child poverty; with a school to prison pipeline that places over 2 million people behind bars; a society where vacant housing is used for tax shelters, while over 6 million people live homeless in the streets; an economy that is based on trillions of dollars for war and the destruction of our environment, while our country's infrastructure crumbles and collapses all around us and jobs that will never return disappear to cheaper markets abroad and the advent of automation; in a country where our Freedom of Speech, Press and Assembly are under attack, the baton is never far away, with thousands of our fellow citizens being killed by the police every year ... and life is always much more uncertain if you are black ... brown ... female ... "other" ....

In times like these dangers and pitfalls abound ... yet, so too do the opportunities, for us, as a people, to unite and stand together in both resistance and solution, to remake our common path – one that puts the well-being of the people and this planet before the profits of a few.

The power to create is in our hands, however if we do not use it the chance may never come again. In times like these, inaction is a sin ... and words can make all the difference.

Mark Lipman, editor
20 January 2017

❖ Line borrowed from the poem, "First They Came," by Pastor Martin Niemöller, Holocaust survivor.

INTRODUCTION
Voices Rising in Power and Unity

There's lots of yeast in these songified poems rising from enraged roads covering those "who will return as millions." Poems written & risen just bullets ago. Poems climbing courthouse poles to bring down konfederate flags. Poems attending lynchings on TV. Poems of Visual hangings. Of People burning.

"Silence is violence so scream."

From tweets to streets, onward/heightsward! Rooftop Revolutionaries mixing "blood cocktails" with PTSD in the soultropoli's allwheres: subways, alleyways, suburbs, sub-divides. From all the ways that the hyper moral stain of religious rites are "funneling humans through the war grinder" – with the help of "Capitalism the religion of greed."

And we're all collateral damage: dauntless workers in doo-rags, flaming factory workers "falling in twisted bunches" from a collapsed fire escape: "edifice of tragedy" after "edifice of tragedy" in "century-old inferno" after "century-old-inferno": rites of women's rights. All this as "a new dream flame[s] from the sun."

Rise is people-powered poetics: a jitney or rickshaw ride of litanies: of crate & cardboard houses, of continuums of hand-me-downs, of breath-taking poems about taking of breaths, of borders that (criss-) cross us, of tear gas & fear gas, of drawing breath & drawing dreams, of hate singing "its sanguine song"/"hate is the heart gone mad," of the sight of "a patrol car [that] still causes an attack of nerves," of the "sexy shackles of debt," of being "Catapulted into the criminal justice system by way of the slavery experience," of labor labor labor in labor, of "I am not sorry for anything I do to free my people," of "Our history … cozied under a blanket full of small pox /Stifled beneath broken treaties," of "colonial scars that shape shifted into alcoholic blissfulness."

Decades apart, New York workers' death rites recall Bangladesh workers' death rites, th/ankhs to pre-ancient rites of poetrees. Giving us news, blues, dues, hues & fuses for our fight with vampires of empires.

"What else could you do to me
that you haven't already done?"

Or, as Jimmy Baldwin put it: "You've taken the best, now take the rest." But you're gonna have to do battle to get it from me. Cause we're "just dying to fight for the future" – and "we're all equal in the face of a riot."

"Somewhere a mother/weeps blood" & everywhere blood weeps for our mothers.

In *Rise, p*oetry's First & what's left to fight with … incendiary & soothful … bomb & balm … *colored* peeps & colorlessness – & color-listed … *real* justice-juiced poetics/aesthetic umpires occupying empires … daily-go-2-meetings … "writin' is fightin'," as Ish Reed puts it … *3rd eye's on the prize.*

Rise-ing poetry is full of "mouths," yes, & "ways" through which struggles usher & much is made to happen. *Rise*-ing poetry is farms & forms: yields of fine & phat words: the brilliantly meshed & the rest – including restively aborning pomes: the polyglottal, the polyphonic, the polymetric-polyrhythmic, the polycultural, the polypsychic, the polywarrior preambles. All polypowered. All yeasting toward Soular Wholes – familistically.

Eugene B. Redmond
Poet Laureate of East St. Louis

EVERY DAY IS AN ANCESTOR'S DAY

To Mama Raimunda and all others
who have made the Transition in the months preceding this poem

Our memories are not for sale
When the ancestors already paid the price
They have walked with us
All over the earth
Every cultural worker, every poet, every working voice

When I cannot write a verse
Without hearing losses of more voices
How *long* to write the dedications?
When a great-grandmother can give birth to a poet
The world trembles
With words of freedom
Spoken in tones of fury
When the time comes
For the poet to return home
The world, with all its words together,
Still cannot tell the story of the loss
As we still tell the stories of their lives
And every day we feel another story
Every day is An Ancestor's Day

Can your heart take more
to hear the news?
They were, no, they are
The voices of people's democracy
We feel pain
Yet we are not broken
They touched our hearts
And felt our pain
Now we go
And carry the flame
On today, yesterday,
Ancestor's Day for every one we honor
In an act of freedom
And for all the names
Now is the time
For the remembering

Ángel L. Martínez

Slavery Behind Counters and Behind Bars

Is it not involuntary servitude
when at home you have no bread
feeding babies are just sweet dreams
while nightmares
are pounding at your head?

Do you feel you're in a prison
when the news tells you that you're free?
Yet all you see is no escape
from incorporated misery.

You make a million every day
and the pennies are all your pay.
Is it not involuntary servitude
for all the wealth you make
for all the money, you've no say?

Is it not the right to rebel
For a march we will walk very far?
Yet remember all the people
Working behind counters and behind bars!

Ángel L. Martínez is Deputy Artistic Director of The Bread is Rising, Poetry Collective, which is celebrating 20 years. He is a poet, professor, singer, cultural worker, and social activist for 25 years.

Ángel L. Martínez

Revolution Blues

My baby didn't get her paycheck
when it was due last week
My baby didn't get her last paycheck,
& neither did the other teachers
The superintendent said "I'm under stress,
please have some empathy!"

To keep your public school,
it only takes a hunger strike
To keep our neighborhood schools open,
it only takes a hunger strike
You might even get the city to remove some lead,
if you ask polite

There's homeless folks on every corner –
some are old, some are in their teens
There's homeless folks on every damn corner –
some are old, some are in their teens
& my people ain't ready for revolution,
naw, they don't even know what it means

Well, Nelson died & I miss him,
& I'm scared for the times ahead,
& my friend Nico died way too early
in his cold hospital bed,
& Donald Trump might win the election,
I heard that in the last poll he's ahead!

Adam Gottlieb

They killed Sandra Bland & then framed her,
& they say the answer is more cops
& they killed those 43 students
down in Ayotzinapa
& it looks like another world war's comin,
    & artists just care about when their project drops

Oh, I got the blues, I got Chicago blues,
yea I got the blues, I got the U.S. blues,
yea I got the blues, globalization blues,
yea I got the blues, civilization blues,
I got the red solution
revolution blues

HERE'S TO THE ROAD
for Nelson Peery

Here's to the road that's been paved by the elders
Here's to the parts of the war they have won,
Here's to the struggle that ever continues
Here's to the living, who must carry on

Nelson was fearless if anyone ever was,
Heart of a soldier, mind beyond measure,
Any words spoken fall painfully short
To describe this great man, and the life that he lived

I am a young person in Nelson's shadow,
Walking the path that he cleared for us all,
I have a body, a mind, and a spirit,
I too have a vision that guides me along

If we are warriors, whether or not we knew him,
All of us here who have walked on his path,
We are all Nelson – his blood flows in our veins –
It's up to us now – we're the world's last chance.

Adam Gottlieb is a poet/emcee, teaching-artist, musician, community organizer, and revolutionary from Chicago. In March 2014 he co-founded the Chicago chapter of the Revolutionary Poets Brigade. He leads a band, "Adam Gottlieb & OneLove." He is also a regular contributor of both poetry and articles to the People's Tribune.

Adam Gottlieb

No Song Can Be Sung

No song can be sung
to dying children
              who will never
              awaken;
No grace given
before an empty table.

The hounds of hell
have driven us out,
the merchants of war
have made us desperate,
the battering rams of hate
lurk like menacing vultures
waiting to take whatever
is left.

No song can be sung;
No grace, however amazing
can be given;
none can be forgiven
as we sit motionless
while they slaughter
our children.

How can we allow
our hearts to keep beating
after witnessing this?
How can we hope to look those who survive
in the eye?

Dorothy "Dottie" Payne

How can we keep turning away
from this holocaust of
all who dare to exist
    without hate in their hearts,
    without money in their pockets,
    without war in their fantasies,
    without the need for greed?

No song can be sung,
no poem written
as long as we
remain silent.

So the strongest among us rise up,
take to the streets,
vow to end
this evil that seeps
into the sheets where
the children sleep
and unsung innocents
can no longer even dream.

This arch of evil
has overreached
borders,
has droned death
relentlessly
and driven us out
into their war zones,
    has made us forego
    begging for what's ours;
    has bent us over once too often,
    left us to bleed fearlessly
    far too many times.

So, we must become hymn and psalm,
make melody of our great green revenge –
we must grace the pages of a New Script
with the diligence of Job.
We too have been put to the tests:
                              our auditions are endless.
                              No symphonies for us,
                              just handshakes, heartaches,
                              and common grace.

They said the boy took
what wasn't his,
defied and pushed back,
and the man flaunted that toy gun
that looked so real –
dared to pretend
he was master of
his own body –
thought he could own
the space around it.

They said the woman
talked back,
used her tongue
like a rapid-fire weapon –
                              had no fear of them –
owned her own mind
up until the very end,
sang her own righteous hymn
heard the world over,
composed our
new world order

as she pure-cursed them
and gasped her last breath,
promised them
their evil was ending
with her heart beat;
                      said they could never
                      silence this.

And they say
she sang
as they strangled her,
first a shriek,
then a muffled little gurgle
turned melodic lisp:

            "This body, this song
              is not yours to own,
                I will return as millions,"

– took her fear
and made it theirs –
raised her eyelids skyward
like a celestial choir –

            hummed young Trayvon's Song,
            gasped Eric Garner's final breath;
            gave her Sandra Bland smile
            as she acapella-vowed
            a retaliation of the spirit
            holier than they could know,
            ancient as a harp.

And we heard it,
heard the whispered symphony
which was her life:
>saw the tracks
>in the snow
>rejoicing
>the arrival of
>our inevitable

>"Hallelujah!"

Dorothy "Dottie" Payne is a poet/artist/culture critic/international educator who has performed her poetry and organized poetry events in Jamaica, the West Indies, San Francisco and St. Louis. She participated in an International Poetry Festival in Havana, Cuba in the summer of 2015. She has run the Art Internationale Gallery and Art Lounge in San Francisco, and served as the artistic director of the Warrior Poets in St. Louis. Her essays have appeared in the St. Louis American, Jakarta Java Kini, Left Curve and Rain Taxi. She has published poems in magazines and anthologies and recently published her first book, Birthmarks. She is member of the internationally acclaimed Revolutionary Poets Brigade.

AMERICA
after Allen Ginsberg

America, I went skiing on your dollar menu,
Sliding down your economic division.
"Such lovely sights," I heard you say.
America, why aren't you here anymore?
Did you send all your tanks to Syria this time?
America, this poem will fuck you 3 times
And 3 times you will deny it is inside you.
America, let's play whirly-ball
On the world stage!
America, did you send all your trees to Canada?
I saw them crossing the green border.
America, did you let Trumpty Dumpty build
His wall across Mexico?
Did you let Pharaoh Carson
Build his pyramids for grain and Jesus?
Why on earth did you let Ted Cruz
Read Green Eggs and Ham to your Senators?
Did you build your factories in Juarez
With the bones you picked from the people?
Why do I sometimes see you hide your head
In the ass of Fox News, America?
You make wa pa pa pa pow sounds
As you hang the poor from the power lines.
America, go build tiny houses in your cities
And give them to those with lampshades for rain coats!
America, go home!
The Lakota are gathering along your pipeline.

Eric Allen Yankee

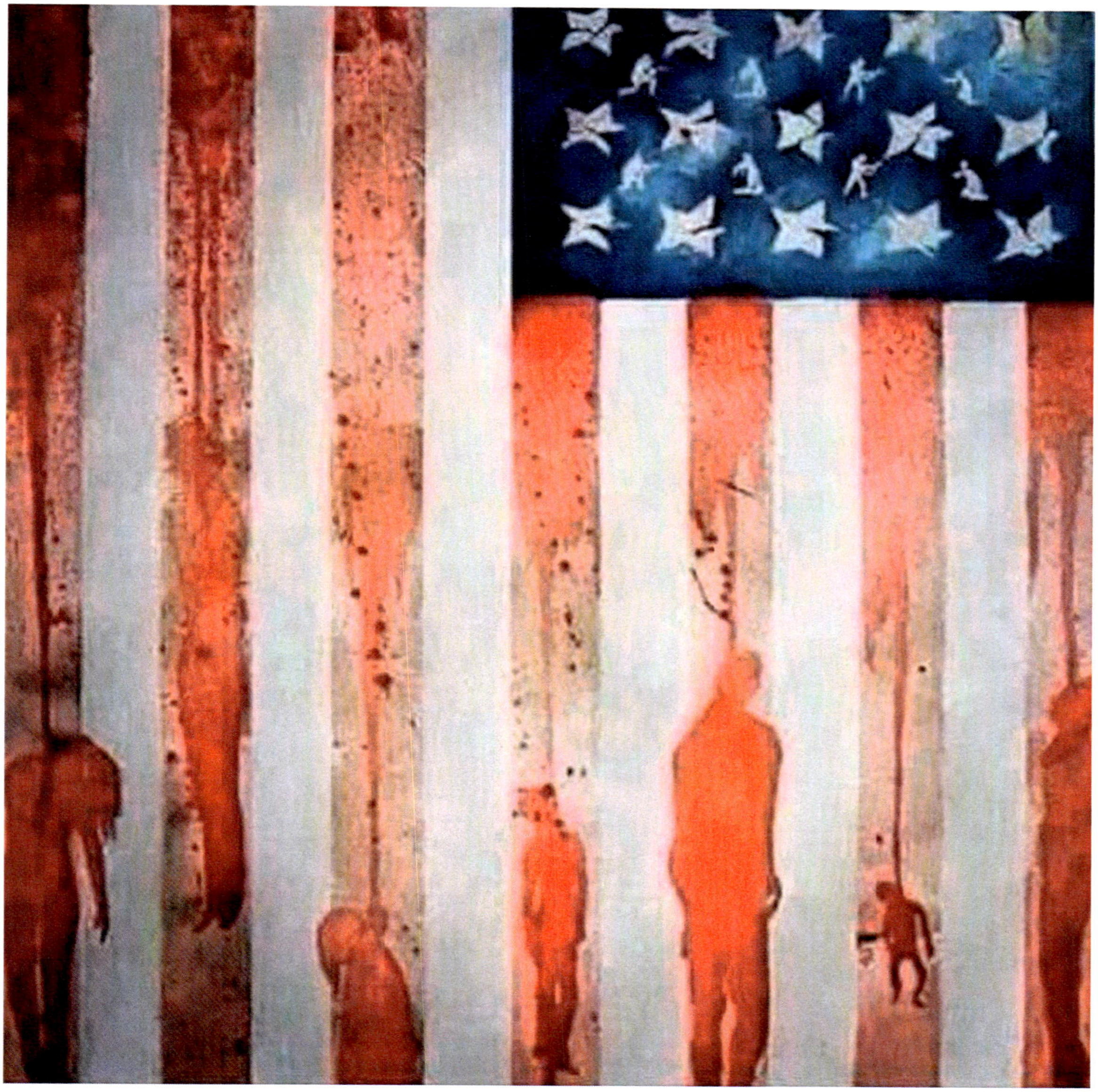

THE DAY AMERICA DIED

On the day America died
A path to peace collapsed
Fires were started in the streets
By government men
In stinking yellow suits
Waving bags of rotting cash
And enticing Black Friday shoppers
Twisted by their desire for a TV

Gas prices went down
As drilling went up
And pipelines destroyed native lands
And America choked
On the blood of the young
Who raised their hands in the air
And were shot anyway
Because no one believes
The young anymore

America is dead
Rebuild the new holy land
We'll start with Detroit
If anyone can turn the water on

Turn the gilded fear back to red
And watch the young die
From behind your screen

Eric Allen Yankee

On the day America died
The colors faded out
And men in bleeding suits
Ran for the gold rush

On the day America died
You and I
Were no longer brothers
In the lost eyes
Of men too deep
Into the war
Of men who read
Fortunes in shell casings
From the bullets
Of Corporate America

On the day America died
You and I died with it
Because we watched
As the young lay bleeding

Eric Allen Yankee is a member of the Revolutionary Poet's Brigade of Chicago. His work appears in *The People's Tribune*, *CC+D*, *Crab fat*, *Ygdrasil*, *The Miscreant*, *Sweet Wolverine*, *Writing Raw*, *The Fem*, and *Overthrowing Capitalism: Volume 2* and has recently been nominated for the prestigious Pushcart Poetry Award. He is also co-editor in chief of *Caravel Literary Arts Journal* (www.caraveljournal.org).

17 Years, 16 Shots

Almost one bullet fired
for every year lost. No
more blowing out candles,
holding another midnight
vigil, the reasons more than
just trivial. Another boy will
never be celebrating any more
birthdays, 17 years and with
16 shots his cake has expired –
as the family gathers to protest,
more than complain, another
headline, another child taken
not kidnapped but executed as
another family left childless
and shaken. Nothing left
but chalk outline of a once
teenage life, left shivering on
concrete silent with all the refrains
haunting Chicago, news shows on
repeat of 16 gun shots scattered
all 17 years over his blood, reasons
never change, how could a child
always be blamed? And why does
anyone triggering blue, hiding
behind a shield, never want
to explain their aim?

Adrian Ernesto Cepeda is an LA Poeta who is currently enrolled in the MFA Graduate program at Antioch University in Los Angeles where he lives with his esposa and their gato Woody Gold. His poetry has been featured in *The Yellow Chair Review*, *Thick with Conviction*, *Silver Birch Press* and one of his poems was named *Cultured Vultures*' Top 3 Poems of the Week. You can connect with Adrian on his website: www.adrianernestocepeda.com

Adrian Ernesto Cepeda

HOW MANY MORE?

What savage times we live in
When cops strike us harder
And protests are built around
Police violence martyrs

Since they single us out
In patrol cars they creep
What officers hath sown,
So shall they reap

Did you ever wonder why
The amount of cop killing rises?
A poor man with a gun
Busts on lawmen he despises

And then comes the wakes
And then comes the burials
Has anyone in your 'hood
Shown up for police funerals?

How many more
Must die
Before the message sinks in?
How many more
Must be buried
Before you recognize their sins?

The defender of your safety
Put Eric Garner in a chokehold
The tragic tales of Grant & Bell
Continue to be told

Tamir Jones never lived
Long enough to see thirteen
Anti-police slogans or killer cops?
Which is more obscene?

The ones you call for protection
The ones you think will serve
The ones you rely on to solve
problems
Leaves most of us unnerved

The court of public
Opinion charges them with genocide
Your dear protectors are legal
Psychos, cut and dried

How many more
Must die
Before the message sinks in?
How many more
Must be buried
Before you recognize their sins?

Dee Allen

REBEL X *for Bree Newsome*

YOU HAVE YOUR X
AND I'LL WEAR MINE

Exclaimed a controversial t-shirt
Back in the Clinton years,
A short open letter
Addressed to the Nubian race

Showcased a battle flag,
The other red, white & blue
Flown in field skirmishes of an ancient
War between split American states.

The last Rhodesian
In South Carolina
Had his X,
Pledged allegiance to it lovingly

Before he opened fire on nine
Black people in a Charleston chapel.
The spirit of Dynamite Bob✣
Worked through him that Sunday morning.

Signifying second-hand
Separation & hate
Passed off as
Honor & heritage, popular amongst

Southern Metal-heads
And gun freaks and
The Ku Klux Klan:

Dee Allen

The Rebel X.

The Courage Award
Shouldn't go to an athlete, but
A woman who, with both hands,
Scaled up a courthouse flagpole and
Removed from the top the region's historic shame:

Emblem of oppression,
Keepsake of a lost cause,
Banner of racism,
Reminder of slavery.

Her action
Indeed took courage

In a state whose
Whiter populace would rather
See its blacker half
Back in chains.

General Lee's seal,
Stars and bars,
The Southern Cross:

The Rebel X.

*Robert Edward Chambliss was a member of United Klans of America & one of four White men responsible for bombing the 16th Street Baptist Church, which caused the death of 4 little Black girls in 1963.

Dee Allen, African-Italian poetry writer and Spoken Word performer currently based in Oakland, California. Allen is active in two San Francisco Bay Area-based Spoken Word performance troupes: Poor Magazine's Po' Poets Project and the Revolutionary Poets Brigade. His first two books *Boneyard* and *Unwritten Law* are both available from Poor Press   www.poormag.info/static/

Dear White Privilege

I know it's not your fault.
And I don't think your guilt will fix the wilt of a mother's soul
who buried a child –
too young to be cold –
no, it's not your fault.
It's not your fault that he shot 9 times
or that his toy gun read thug in that cop's mind –
it's not your fault that the high strung, sense dumb and mind numb fired shots
into a crowd, seconds later, a 22 year old girl, dead on the ground.
It's not your fault that the mentally ill, choking on a racist bitter pill was
beaten then shot for sleeping on a bench because this day in age, you call a
cop when you want someone lynched.
It's not your fault.
It's not your fault that he went in, just a kid and then –
three years of your worst fears realized in the prime
of what could have been a long life –
no conviction named for affliction sustained, a valediction framed in the
remains of a 22 year old boy. No, this is not your fault.
It's not your fault that your skin is light
but understand how painful shades of grey do crumble
neath the hooded lady justice claiming
black
or right.
A thug is created, just like a man –
and when poverty's planned, minorities scanned –
to read trouble, from school to prison – anywhere in this land,
is it any wonder that more black men are in prison now than were slaves?

Eleanor Goldfield

And I'd comment on black women too –
save that stats are lacking cuz that's 2 strikes against you –
black and a woman, too?
Shit YOU – a white man won't understand
but that doesn't mean that a white hand –
can't make a fist, raised to the sky, stand on the front lines, always an ally –
you're not outside, this is your system too –
twisted, amiss a corporate abyss –
if your skin's a slip –
thru the system, golden ticket – get out of jail –
free –
let's see –
is that ok with you?
It's not ok with me –
that skin is a caste –
system, a class –
tear it off and we all bleed.
Now do you see?
Our white privilege isn't your fault, isn't mine or my parents –
but to look in the mirror and think it's all fair
cuz you have a black friend and kinks in your hair,
step off the white box and stare.
Stare at this system, a cold honest glare –
no, it's not fair, and it's not your fault.
But now we can see and it will be our fault if we stay, wrapped in our skin,
shrug and say hey, not my fault.

Now, it is.
Silence is violence so scream.
Scream not because you know how it feels
but because you know what it means to
not be free –
and none of us will be free
till all of us stand up
and scream.

Eleanor Goldfield is a creative activist, singer and writer. She is the founder and lead singer of the political hard rock band, Rooftop Revolutionaries who have shared the stage with the likes of Tom Morello and Immortal Technique at festivals, Occupy events and rock clubs around the country. She is also the host and writer of the occupy.com, Free Speech TV syndicated show, Act Out! which focuses on creative and grassroots activism. This weekly show gives updates on activism around the country, focusing on artists and creatives, grassroots actions and how people anywhere can get involved, from tweets to marching in the streets. She is also a free-lance writer and consultant for creative outreach targeting 18-30 year olds via projects aimed at killing apathy through art. In this capacity, she also does various creative work on her own, such as her campaign, Ads for Change.
rooftoprevolutionaries.com   occupy.com/actout   artkillingapathy.com

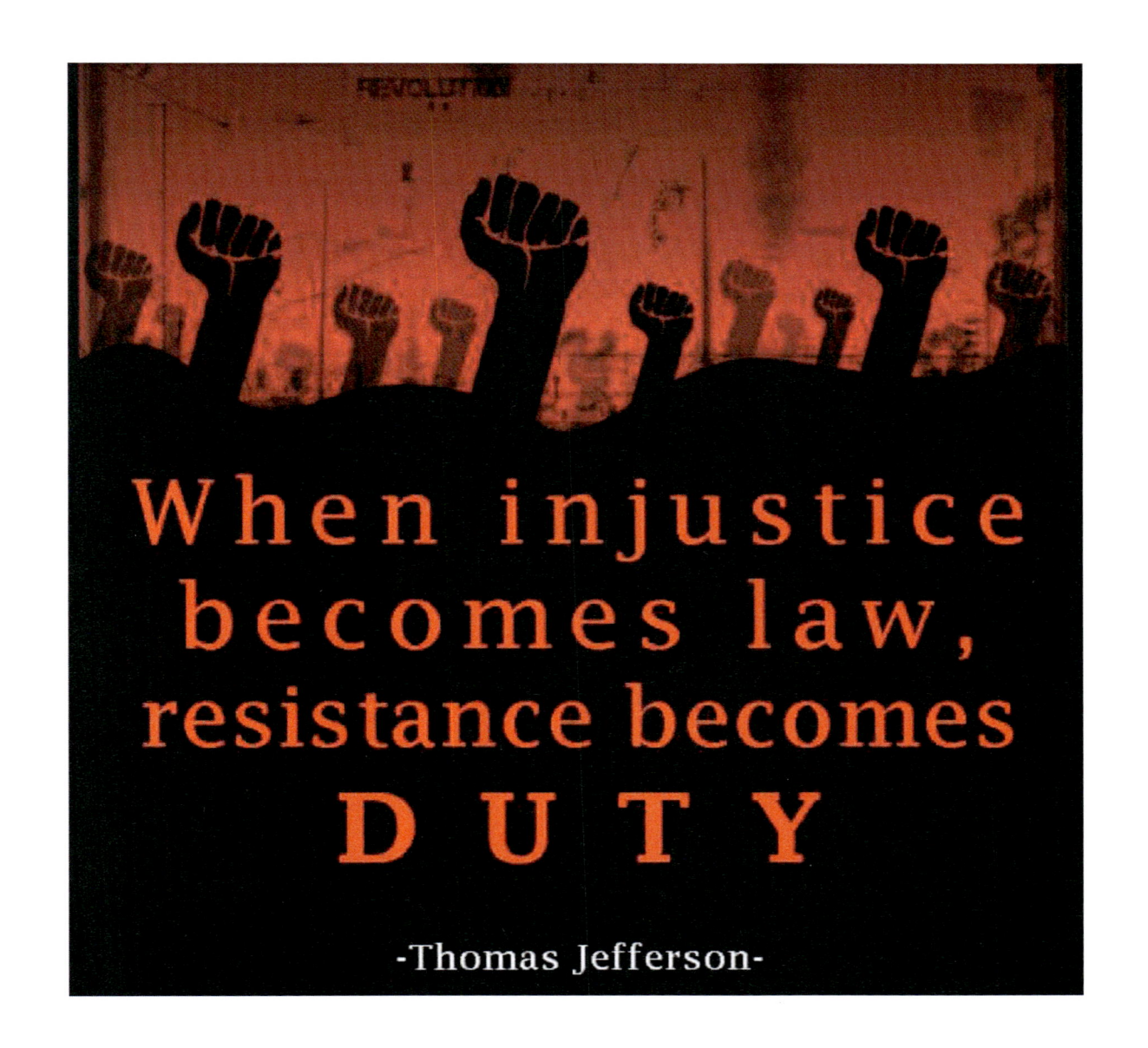

When injustice becomes law, resistance becomes DUTY

-Thomas Jefferson-

WE ARE RISING

4:45am
4 hours of sleep
I get ready for work
And let my son sleep a little longer
Before our 12 hour day
Knowing all of our children
Deserve more
Than crumbs
Knowing that all people
Who rise to work
Deserve more
Than what they are given
We are rising
Single mother
Welfare lines
Health clinics
You learn
Medi-cal means medi-can't
Red tape looks like this
30 minute phone calls to change doctors
Just to hear them say
You got to go to urgent care
20 minutes away
Instead you decide on
A two hour wait
And in that time I think about how
They tell you
You make your decision
But you don't have a choice
You have to pay for this office visit today

Irene Monica Sanchez

You learn when you ask for help
You will pay and they'll punish
As they charge you sliding scale
For a clinic outside the one they changed you to
When you always went to this one
20 dollars you don't have
And you pay
More than 20 dollars
And you pay
A day worth of lost wages
Maybe two
And you pay
Because you have no other choice
This is your son
You think to how you lost your food stamps this month
And the new paycheck isn't coming on time
And now you missed work in your first month
A half paycheck is coming
But not soon enough
And it's not enough
Will it ever be enough?
For you to find a new place to live for you and your son to live and be
We just want to be happy, healthy, and free to be …
But there is no shelter here
You've seen the inside of DV shelters
Wondering if you deserve their help and
You come to places to stand in welfare lines and
They have you wondering
If you deserve help
You come back to your hometown
After ten years
And they leave you wondering
If you deserve their help

And you remember why you left
So instead of help
Some offer you prayers
As if that will give you a roof over your head
Or food to eat
Their capacity for compassion lasts about an hour on Sunday
And they pray for you
To a God you no longer trust
Because they want you to pay for prayers too
Nothing comes for free here
You will pay for this charity they applaud themselves for
And they will punish
By making you beg for mercy on your knees
I wonder what Jesus would say?
They say all of us are a paycheck or two away from being homeless
I think it's half a paycheck
But they say we single mothers on welfare
Abuse the system
That we pay dearly into
Never paying attention to the ways in which
Capitalism, Patriarchy and Misogyny
Has abused us
Our whole lives
So don't give me crumbs
I am coming to collect my bread
That we harvested
And the rumble in my belly reminds me
I am not only in need of food stamps
To eat
This rumble is the reason I rise
Everyday
I am hungry for justice

The "Latina" is the
lowest paid worker in the U.S.
54 cents
But we all have equal opportunity
In this land of the free
Home of the brave
California so liberal they barely repealed
A law criminalizing women on welfare
That placed a cap on how many kids a woman can have
As if the extra 130 dollars is worth this time
Standing in welfare lines for crumbs
These safety nets
Are full of holes
In this system if you fall
You hit concrete
And with broken limbs you are told as people walk on by
"No one owes you a goddamn thing
This is America
You will pay and we will punish"
But we are rising
And I won't accept these crumbs
We are coming to collect loaves of bread
To feed our children
We are coming to take over the factories and
The fields
To feed our children
And we are hungry for justice

Dr. Irene Monica Sanchez completed a M.Ed. and Ph.D. in Educational Leadership and Policy Studies and a graduate certificate in Feminist Studies. She continues to advocate for underserved populations in higher education and in society at large for immigrant and workers rights as well as causes dedicated to ending gender based violence. Irene was a member of M.E.Ch.A. (RCC & UW) and a member of the Autonomous Chapter of the Watsonville Brown Berets.

American Spring

I. With grains of good intention they feed us
hysterics through flat screens; worship
Big Brother – the all-seeing eye;
take Somas; repeat.

II. Repetition –
Bernays' democratic persuasion to
concoct a potion – panic-propaganda –
& streamline it straight into the bloodstream
of Industrial America.

III. "A toast," they say, "to the frenzy… *Freedom!*"
clink with blood cocktails; (there's an America, dying
to be reborn – *yes we can* – diluted ideologies
that still surge in the veins of its people).

IV. Whitewashed bones cracking
on the periphery of a new day;
Pearl Harbor,
9/11,
the Invasion of Normandy;
pump terror into America's heartland; placate the masses
with violent distraction. We are tired
of death; of funneling humans through the war grinder

V. Unknowing last notes from 19 year old soldiers
to mothers scattered across suburbs. Memorials –
an open wound; fathers ruminating services
for the mangled limbs of sons & daughters.

Anmarie Soucie

VI. So, crouching low on building's rooftops, interspersed
 throughout the cities of this blood-soaked land, we lie in wait,
 to cut through the wire of coded phrases; political
 trickery; the two party system of one scam; pay attention
 to PTSD; the limbless veterans who
 hang dollar signs
 on subway stoops;

VII. (High above the Metropolis, they nod in towers, palming medals;
 eyes averted to man-made constructions – tattered maps of territories,
 religious artifacts, the stain of morality).

VIII. But we, fidgeting,
 pick at our lip's dried stitches
 – our generation, a trembling chrysalis;
 and wait for the sound when
 the gestation period
 (two hundred and fifty-two)
 closes, and a new day
 stirs.

Anmarie Soucie is a writer/performer living in New York City's Lower East Side. She received a BA in humanities – creative writing and literature – from New York University, and is completing her first novel, *Broken Jade*.

IRON CLAW
in memory of Trayvon Martin

There is no song in a gun
this time it's aimed
into the mouth of the night
where our conscience lies
in the blood stained grass
beneath his dark skin and hoodie
and the bullet hole left in his heart

There is no song in a gun
this time its stolen your tongue
your words a tellurium of rain
steel hollowed tips
penetrating flesh and bone

There is no song in a gun
this time just the deafening sound
piercing the wind in
a murderous scream
wiped out by the lie
of a beautiful here and after

There is no song in a gun
No harmony
No melody to hum
Only dissonant cries
in the dimmest of nights
Only bigoted hands
taking too many lives.

Anika Paris

Bullets in the Sky

Ever wonder what we keep fighting for
I don't know who's keeping score but I
know too many Kings have build a lawn of graves
or a wall with many names

Ashes to ashes and dust to dust
it's the killing fields for all of us

And she cries while bullets in the sky
fall down like rain, and we watch
ten million miles away now who's to blame
There's a fire burning down
this masquerade of hopes and dreams,
bloody streets and children's screams
We will never know it, they will never show it
Bullets fall like rain

Who are we to judge
if freedom's in your hands
what color of the skin makes up a man
Can't we all agree
should there be a God above
what happened to his love

Ashes to ashes and dust to dust
The killing fields for all of us

Anika Paris

And she cries while bullets in the sky
fall down like rain, and we watch
ten million miles away now who's to blame
There's a fire burning down
this masquerade of hopes and dreams,
bloody streets and children's screams
We will never know it, they will never show it
Bullets fall like rain

Anika Paris is a platinum award winning singer/songwriter with songs in major motion pictures and television. As a composer, her work was featured in multiple theatre productions in New York City for MultiStages and the League of Professional Theatre Women including; the award-winning The Island of No Tomorrows, The Judas Tree, Novel, HOLA Award Winner "Temple of the Souls" with co-writer Dean Landon, for MultiStages; and Morpho-Genesis. She teaches songwriting and performance at UCLA, the Grammy and Musicians Institute, and is a published authored of two books *Making Your Mark in Music* and *Five Star Music Makeover* with Hal Leonard. As a poet, she has appeared the Kansas City Star, Helicon Nine Editions, Gival Press, Whirly Bird Press, Half-Shell Press, and most recently with Scapegoat Press in a three generation anthology *Woven Voices* alongside her mother and grandmother, which was nominated for the International Latin Book Award.

The American Machine

In the America I live in,
Much is made of the American gangster

This is why "Scarface" and "The Godfather"
Don't leave weekly cable tv rotation

But it also spreads to the famous
American notion of success –
"The dream"

In which everyone must
Start from nothing to gain something

Even seen in the way Americans laud
The born-into-it big timer
As long as he served a summer stint at McDonalds
Or if he in any other way devoted himself
To a great American franchise

I am not generalizing but absolutely do mean
"he"
Because the American dream
Provides different avenues for a female
She comes up not from common labor and pluck
But out of motherhood
Sexual abuse
Or decades of marriage

What I mean is we like to see the men –
Businessman
Politician

M. A. Peterson

Entrepreneur
Eccentric

Who we can say understands
The value of the American dollar
(our values)
Because he has dabbled temporarily
In what could be described as
"struggling"
The issue here is that
I've had many friends and acquaintances
Who had plenty of pluck
Good luck
Worth ethic
And strike-it-rich intentions

And yet never made it above
Floor manager
Head server
Key holder
Opening supervisor

Or some other condescending stunt
That clearly was meant to say
You are better than average
But should be paid
Only slightly above average

I have known so many people
That worked hard and were willing
To work harder
Who worked a 70 hour work week
On a meager salary check that was designed
To abuse them

I have known many men and women
Who kept as keen to 70 hours a week schedules
As a well sharpened knife
Hoping it could cleave them to ease and a better income

While a life of ease remains a needle head
That almost no one threads

Some of the hardest working people I've known
Were single mothers and ex-convicts
Who worked on factory assembly lines
After eventually coming to understand
That much like in grade-school sports
Non-participation in the American economy
Is more despised than failure to succeed

(The American dream is a deliberate machine
That produces citizens who are prepared
To do whatever it takes to succeed in some way
The gangster no different from the lawmaker
From the paid lover
From the president
From the CEO
From the distributer
From the boy at 14 first learning to con with an innocent smile

To chase this dream is to admit one's self
To a series of self-degradations
That may prove to be endless

But just may prove in the end
That you are worthy to degrade others)

50

THE OVER-EMPLOYED

In America,
We like to classify our levels of destitution –
The news will often report the rates of homelessness,
The un-employed, the under-employed...
I'd like to add to this hopeless list
The over-employed.
Those who excel at scraping by,
Who get confused by a day off,
Whose car/bus bag is full of hangers
From switching uniforms between jobs,
Who feel like it's a luxury to eat a meal sitting down.

This category of people don't do "Well."
They are mostly too busy to "get ahead,"
"luck out," or "take advantage of opportunity."

Instead they get/luck/take
Shopper's discount promotions,
Government programs,
And public transportation.

We may not have what you could mark on an application
As "special skills,"
But we know how to cook dried beans into something
That seems elaborately planned.
We know how to get on our knees in front of a bathtub
And wash our clothes by hand.

M. A. Peterson

We know a dozen alternate ways to make money
If/when our second or first jobs fall through (again).

We are the elite set of humans that never get up very high
Yet always end up having to land on our feet.

We work hard so your statistics don't have to.

M. A. Peterson is an anthropology graduate student, permaculturist, independent radio and museum volunteer, and waitress.

Women on Fire

It was a cold, unpleasant day
In New York, that gray March 25, 1911,
But the old Asch building at MacArthur and Greene
Squared its concrete shoulders, and shrugged off the chill.

High above, on the eighth through tenth floors,
The women inside were unaware of the weather;
It belonged to the outside world, off-limits to them
Until the first shadows of night.

Their world consisted of the windowless walls
Of the Triangle Shirtwaist factory,
Whose young employees cut and sewed blouses
By the thousands for seven to twelve dollars a week.

Somewhere on the eighth floor,
A fire took form then unstoppable life,
In a scrap bin holding the detritus of sweatshop labor.
Hundreds of pieces of bright cloth and fabric
Lay uncollected and forgotten,
Just like the women who turned them into something beautiful.

When the burning began, a frantic call from the eighth floor
Gave warning to those on the tenth,
But the ninth floor was already ablaze
Like the Ninth Circle of Hell.
The fire consumed as it climbed,
Spreading orange fingers toward a fearsome embrace
With the frantic survivors on the roof.
There were elevators, but they were full within minutes.

Henry Howard

There were exit doors,
But the owners kept them locked during working hours
To prevent unauthorized breaks,
Or thefts of the sacred cloth,
Or the forbidden fruit of cigarettes, smoked through the fabric.
There was a fire escape, old and unreliable
As the factory owners themselves,
And it soon collapsed under the weight of bodies
Who clung to it like grapes, until falling in twisted bunches
To the scorched pavement below.

Soon there was but one way out
For the dozens of women and men
With no earthly exit.

One by one
Or two by two,
Holding hands to give them courage,
Women and girls appeared at the crackling windows,
Young Jewish and Italian immigrants willing to climb
The ladder of success rung by rung
Through the horror of sweatshop labor.

Of the 123 women and 23 men consumed by the Triangle fire,
Sixty two ushered in the era of jumpers:
A man was seen kissing a woman in silhouette,
Before they were married to the flames.

There was little Kate Leone
And her best friend Sarah Rosario Maltese,
14-year-year olds whose short lives
And long journey to America
Ended in a fierce embrace beneath a blanket of fire.

By the end of the long day,
The last embers twinkled in the breeze
Like the glow of freshly-lit cigarettes,
And mingled with the soft gray ash and even whiter snow
To lend a cloak of dignity to the charred forms
On the cobblestones far below.

They were the first, these sixty two jumpers,
But they have not been the last.
When the World Trade Center crumbled
In the terror attacks of 9/11,
There were those who cheated death from above
By taking a long leap into eternity.

There was the office worker, who placed a forlorn call
To his wife of three decades,
Only to find her answering machine on;

There was the master chef in the restaurant
Called Windows on the World,
Who cooked a fabulous omelet for the last time
Before jumping from the frying pan to escape the fire;

And there was the young woman,
Whose death jump was caught forever in a freeze-frame image
Of an awful moment in time:
In a last-ditch effort to preserve her dignity,
She straightened her skirt and tugged it modestly
Over panties no one could see but her.

No one can begin to grasp what it was like
To open the smoke-stained windows
And gaze at the world far below,
Before slipping the bonds of earth

And riding the wind on wings of eagles.
The endless days of burning steel and nights of broken glass
Were my generation's Triangle Fire.

When I was a student at NYU,
I took a statistics class in that long-ago death factory
And never knew where I was,
For the desks and sewing machines had been replaced
By chalkboards and overhead projectors,
And not even a memorial plaque adorned this edifice of tragedy.

Some good actually came from that century-old inferno.
Dozens of progressive laws sprouted like mushrooms
Across the conscience of the labor landscape:
A shorter workweek, better pay, greater safety,
And a strong new union to fight for it all.

It was a blaze that sparked an unquenchable movement
Of worker's rights and women's rights.
But why does it still take,
From the remote factories of Bangladesh
To the modern sweatshops that rise unseen
In the high-rises of Los Angeles,
Women on fire to spread flames of justice
That will never die?

Henry Howard is a Los Angeles Peace Poet, and a proud member of the Revolutionary Poets Brigade. He has recently written a second volume of poetry, published by VAGABOND, called *Sing to Me of My Rights*, which won the Silver Award in the *Evergreen Medal for World Peace*, as part of the *Independent Book Publishers Awards*. Yes, indeed: if we sing loudly enough to people of their human rights, they will learn the tune and sing it loudly enough for themselves to break the chains of their own, and other people's oppression. All the truly great revolutions in history have started with great words!

We Are All Jimmy Baldwin

In the Village of Harlem

Slowly the moon is rising on this Saturday cloudy morning
on this month of August. As I sat in the dining room listening to WBGO
like every Saturday to the Felix Hernández show like a blast from the past.
The phone rang at 10 o'clock. It was Jabril to tell me he will meet me in front
of the building at 12 noon.
The time passed when in minutes the bell rang,
I walked down from my apartment over to the lift and pressed the button
and went in down to meet him by the stoop, greeted each other con paz,
and walked over towards the hill on Park Avenue.
The sidewalk was crowded as the people were gathering en La Plaza de la Marqueta
to their weekly dance of guaguancó. We stopped for a few seconds on our way
toward 123rd Street and Madison Avenue.
We entered into Marcus Garvey Park and took the shortcut. We passed children
who were playing in the pool. The homeless were sleeping on the benches and some
were playing chess or dominoes.
Finally we reached the corner of 5th Avenue and 124th Street. We crossed the street
over to 125th Street.
Besides the corner there was a vendor who was selling oil and incense and shea
butter and myrrh and frankincense. We greeted each other with peace to the world
of Jimmy's Harlem.
It was in the middle of the Depression, the rat-infested tenements, men and women
and children were scratching in the garbage cans for food, foraging with cats and
the dogs. The long bread lines, the soup kitchens. The people were surviving selling
wood to their neighbors to heat the cold water flats.
People were selling newspapers and shoe-shining and shopping bags to bring food
for their house.
And at times, all you can eat at Father Divine's Restaurant for 15 cents.

Carlos Raúl Dufflar

Sweet Daddy's Church fed the people.
Jimmy came at age at seven. The people were facing starvation with a few chances that Jesus will lead the way but welfare will feed us. Harlem was marching and protesting for jobs and justice.
Don't buy where you can't work.
The people's campaign
The Harlem Rebellion of 1935 as Lino Rivera, 16 years old, was brutally beaten at the S H Kress store as the people were sick and tired of segregation and Discrimination, pains of hunger and unemployment.
Jimmy was ten at that time when the Garvey movement was rising from the spirit against colonialism with love.
From the winds of change the African Blood Brotherhood that laid the seed of consciousness for a new world without capital oppression: jobs, justice, and freedom. From the bitter pains of poverty and homelessness, racist dungeon, lack of health care.
Harlemites were struggling to make ends meet from the wings of the liberals and the NAACP and the Communist Party USA.
Power makes things happen, fighting to defend families who have been evicted from the slumlords, from the miserable conditions, demanding employment for the people of Harlem, for public housing and justice and peace.
The cry and protest against injustice and education had the largest voice in the hearts of Harlemites.
Rally to save the Scottsboro boys as the people lifted their voices.
And Adam Clayton Powell was elected to Congress.
Benjamin Davis was elected Communist councilperson
And a new dream flamed from the Sun.
The kitchen workers, the servants, the printers, the subway workers,
the factory workers beneath the blues of all those years the trumpet sounds celebrated a mighty victory.

Jimmy grew from the pains and the sorrows that the working class lived. It brought the light of consciousness for the old Harlemites daring to dream and write and struggle for human rights and social justice and love and to free the Harlem Six.
And finally, we walked over towards the crowd that formed alongside of his former school, PS 124, of 128th Street between 5th Avenue and Madison Avenue to honor our own native son after decades that went by.
As they proclaim James Baldwin Day, the crowd cried "We are all Jimmy Baldwin" four times.
They placed the sign at Jimmy Baldwin's Place in the front of the building.
Like an old doo wop song of yesterday, only years change into new. Like Life is But a Dream by The Harptones of Harlem.
But Harlemites are under siege: public housing and tenements and cardboard houses and park benches under the bridge and doorways, racist mass police brutality, charter public schools,, mass unemployment and underemployment, lack of affordable housing, food insecurity, as big mouthed politicians are selling the neighborhood short for chump change as the settlers are arriving like a white knight, gentrification, vacant lots rising into condominiums, brownstones and big stores have arrived.
The wretched of the earth must be heard
but our notes for our ancestors we must listen to the circle
that our struggle stays on.
Prepare for the road as the drumbeats shall be treasured.
And when there's no justice, there's no peace.
With love and passion and faith, we will never be shaken.
And Jimmy's blues, the flame in our heart for a new tomorrow like Notes of a Native Son, la lucha continues.
Jimmy está presente.

Asere Bill Epton

A Song be Remembered

When the Earth changes
into red leaves
Comrade Bill was born
in the Village of Harlem
over the eyes
and behind the moon clouds
the flames of working class
stood its ground
a wave of drums
approaches over a blue spirit
at every corner of each
block you hear the street rhythms
in the stoops and the blood of
heart to the heart
after centuries the people being
held in the cages of the hell hole
capitalism exploitation
the empire's imperialist
wars in Vietnam and at home
Comrade Bill was guided with
science of struggle of Marx and Lenin
and Mao and Love
Mother's Mothers are mourning
the death of the children that are lost in the
memories of police brutality
slumlords living in dog heaven
in the unholy mask of colonialism

Carlos Raúl Dufflar

and when mercenaries drank the
blood of young James Powell
on the hot summer of 1964
the thunder of the people
woke up in an earthquake
from the communion of corporations
Comrade Bill founded the
Afro American Labor Council
Founder and Vice President of the
Progressive Labor Party and
The Black Radical Congress
and the Citywide Coalition to Stop Rudy Giuliani
as all poems begin
hold on to our banner
for proletarian reunion
Presente!

Carlos Raúl Dufflar is Founder and Artistic Director of The Bread is Rising, Poetry Collective, which is celebrating 20 years. He is a poet, playwright, cultural worker, and social activist for about 50 years.

I Come from Trash

It's true. I come from trash.
I come from classism, racism, sexism, and from spell check.
It's true.
The computer underlines my esoteric words.
But, still, I come from trash.
I come from manipulation.
I come from a genius of manipulation.
I come from jealousy, greed, hate, and admiration of the skies
that I don't belong to.
I come from an evil patriarchal faith.
And, I was sold for ten pieces of gold.
I know!
I was such a very expensive child.
But some people knew my worth at age 7.
I was such a bilingual child.
Why, I could read Spanish by age 7.
They took a chance on me.
And, I was worth it.
I mean, how many aliens can you get in a room for nothing?
So, I go to my Mama – the Ocean.
She says, "Good things will come about once you tell the truth."
But since I am a loyal and faithful creature,
I say nothing.
Why, I lie.
I lie so bad.
People think me a Goddess.
People think me royalty.

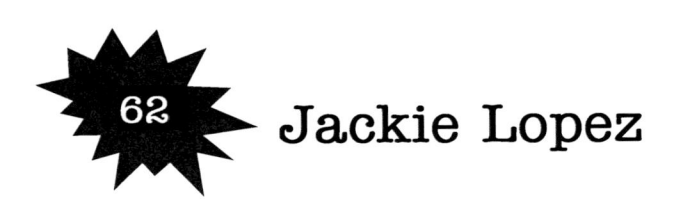

Jackie Lopez

Why, it is because I am a royal woman full of candor and love for all those who surround me.
My evil faith, you see, is showing love and kindness to the sociopaths.
Why, they say a nation is an empire.
But, I say, some people are empires.
They are imperialistic and demand service.
To these people, I have given goodness, gladness, kindness because they suffer from ineptitude.
They just don't know how to handle a good thing when they see it.
I mean, there are tons and tons of people suffering
from empires and everyday people.
But, as you know, I am a poet.
Such things do happen.
So, next time, you see me walking down the street say,
"No one can steal your flight!"
I know.
Such things have been said before.

But I am told that I am eternal wait.
And, there happens to be a mountain of loneliness waiting for me.
In the meantime, know that I come from racism, classism, and sexism-trash.
And, I can't wait to get out of this bin.

Love is Stronger than Hate: Poem for the Ages

God pulled me aside and said,
"An enlightened person can reach 650,000 people at a time."
They say that hate contracts you and only creates a mob.
Well, a long time ago, a raging mob crucified a man.
And, after 2,000 years, this man is still remembered.
He was one man.
Lost and lonely, I still have love.
I have my little heart that loves the Chicanos, Blacks, Puerto Ricans,
Filipinos, Irish Americans, Native Americans and all.
So, hum.
Breathe in and out –
that no matter what the outcome, there are more of us than those that hate.
If it took me a lifetime to meet you, then here I am.
If I were to wear my garments of poetry for the occasion, so be it.
I know that love is stronger than hate.
And, by the Gods and Goddesses, I am in love.
I sway the masses with a dance.
I'm solemnizing the occasion.
A poem is sweet when the morning comes.
A poem is better when midnight hits town.
Give a little look-see up my dress and find a tie.
I know that I shouldn't say such things,
But I was taught in the school of hand-me-downs.
I was the washer woman.
I was the poet in the laundromat.
I took care of my little brothers.
I took good care of my soul.

Jackie Lopez

I got a chance to be enlightened, and I took it like a thieving mistress off of
El Cajon Blvd.
They say that a job like mine should only exist for those that have money.
I say, it only takes love to live so richly.
I am the Gypsy, Poet, immigrant, house cleaner, gardener,
the color-coordinated model.
I know how to spell ice cream, and I have myself some
before they take me away under the guise of some Fascist law.
I pray to all those who have love in their hearts to sing and dance and write
and play and paint and perform.
I know I am not the only theatre in town.
I know that there is magic in the air.
And, that soon we will all look back at these days as the dark ages.
Love is infectious and it has me combing my hair.
So, hum.
Love is when the moon gives you breakfast and the sun gives you dinner.

Jackie Lopez is an activist poet, in mostly, Southern California. She has read for Janice Jordan, border activists, Centro Cultural de la Raza, The World Beat Center, N.O. W., and many other venues for over 20 years. She was founding member of historic troupe, "The Shop Poets." She is a UCSD graduate and graduate school for her consisted of time in The New School for Social Research in New York and at SDSU in San Diego. She experienced a spiritual awakening in graduate school and dropped out only to join a writers' group called "Cabin 20" headed by Luis Alberto Urrea. He is still her mentor and has learned much about writing through this remarkable mentee/mentor relationship. Her spiritual awakening transformed her into a mystic poet but one still in keeping with activism. Her journey has been one of a persistent search of truth, courage, magic, research, ecstasy, enlightenment, and pain in an unequal world. Her poems always end in faith that the light shall always overcome the darkness. She has been published in "La Bloga" eight times, "The Hummingbird Review" twice, "The Border Crossed Us (an anthology to end apartheid)" and other Literary journals. "La Bloga" selected one of her poems for the "Best of 2015 La Bloga Edition." peacemarisolbeautiful@yahoo.com
Facebook: Jackie Lopez Lopez in San Diego.

66

LITANY FOR PEACE

Pick up a rock.
Set it down.

Pick up a rock.
Set it down.

Backs bowed.
Eyes to ground.
Set it down.

Eyes to ground become embers
Inflame the underbrush.
Set it down.

Lit underbrush, hot brush
Cracks open forests.
Set it down.

Across the field
We can only watch.
We each have a right to exist.

We live our lives on cold streets
Crave homes of our own. No school,
No hospital, no ministry of justice
Is impervious to flame.

Set it down. Set it down.
Set it down. NOW.

Elizabeth Marino is a Chicago-based poet, educator and activist, a member of the local Revolutionary Poets Brigade, and has work in the new anthology, *Smash Capitalism Vol. II.* Her poems have appeared internationally and locally in print anthologies, journals and online. Her two chapbooks (*Debris: Poems & Memoir*: Puddin'head Press and *Ceremonies*: dancing girl press) are still in print.

Painting of Elizabeth Marino by Daniel Cleary

Elizabeth Marino

ABUSE OF POWER

for 18-year old Federico Aldrovandi beaten to death by 3 policemen and a policewoman

Power and abuse. I don't love these words,
not even the abuse of power or those who detain
it. Badge, uniform, billy club, fire gun. These aren't
things that make me feel safe as I walk in the streets.

– Look at me! When I walk, I am harmless. When you stop me,
I am harmless. When you handcuff me, I am harmless. When you
force me to kneel down, I am harmless. When you pin me down to
the ground with your weight, I am harmless. When you beat me, I am
harmless. When I turn against you as a bird in a fowler's snare, I am harmless.
As I scream out of the pain you inflict me, as I keep retching, I am

harmless!

Here I am. A swollen face on the asphalt, a living – soon dying –
bruise. If this is what you call justice, I might have to study again
the meaning of the word, tonight. Justice is my bones smashed by
your billy clubs. Justice is my heart's hematoma. Justice is my fifty-four
wounds and bruises. Justice is my traumatic brain injury. Justice is this
bed of blood, this magenta shroud on which I lie. So, in this black dawn, I die as
my namesake, Federico Lorca, executed at sunrise on August 19th (nineteen-
thirty-eight), by Francoists. Murdered by law and order men and women that
still today wear, each and every morning, their uniform filthy with

                                                                justice!

Alessandra Bava is a poet and a translator. Her poems and translations have appeared or are upcoming in journals such as Gargoyle, Plath Profiles, THRUSH and Waxwing. She has recently received her second Best of the Net nomination. Two of her chapbooks, *They Talk About Death* and *Diagnosis*, have been published in the States. She is currently writing the biography of a contemporary American poet.

Alessandra Bava

AND I SAY POWER TO THE PEOPLE
after the PBS Black Panther Party Documentary

i am a revolutionary. i am, a revolutionary.
my afro sits proud on my head,
my fist bald tight on my wrist raised to the sky,
beautiful,
militant,
a reflection of my flag, and my people, and my blood
i am the blood of the 60's.
the midnight raids and gun fights,
flashing light bombs boom with tear gas
my eyes scorch with fire from the depths of Chicago
my lungs suffocate like the bodies in Oakland,
I am everywhere and won't be kept silent.

i am a revolutionary. i am, a revolutionary.
i am the black brotha, black sista and child,
black grandparent, and uncle
i am jive turkey and foxy lady
i am foxy
a fox
a wanted animal for my fur.
my fur don't look that good round necks no,
it looks best being man handled by the white man
the white man know how to cut, gut, and clean a nigga.
these pigs are carnivores standing tall on the human food chain
and I refuse to allow my brothas and sistas to be slaughtered.
I won't go down without a fight.

i am a revolutionary. i am, a revolutionary.
my people are my strength, are my community

Tim Hall

i carry them through the streets,
through the hoods and ghettos, the schools and playgrounds.
i feed and educate the children, inspire the men and women
i get high on my people
i love my people
the people are my power and I say power to the people
power, to the people.

my people are tired of the U.S. political system,
the surveillance, infiltration, perjury, and police harassment,
the trickery to pit my people against one another.
the use of informants and scare tactics to find weaknesses in my people's army has resulted in hundreds of deaths,
and for what?
well i'll tell you,
for fear that the negro community has had enough of the White man's control, of the White man's power.
this ain't nothing new y'all,
this been goin' on for generations.
genocide of my people's ancestors flare in their nostrils
as they march through the streets,
itch my people's trigger finger waiting for the pig to pop off,
keep in my people's tears from the coffins made by this movement
this movement is needed.
ain't no way my people gone be slave again,
my people be free negros,
free with minds enlightened
free with guns cocked and organized
free with communities banded together around the globe
free to speak, vote, and live in a world without fear of being black

my people be revolutionaries, i am a revolutionary. say it with me y'all,
i am a revolutionary, i am a revolutionary, i am, a revolutionary.

Autumn Leaves

To live in this skin,
Is to fear breathing,
Is to have no control of breathing,
Is to walk around with two puffs left in my inhaler,
hesitant to use it,
worried that I won't be able to breathe someday.

To live in this skin,
Is to scream with no one listening,
Is to bruise easily
Is to bleed easily
Is to die easily.

To live in this skin,
Is to walk and be watched,
Is to grow eyes in the back on my head,
Is to be seen always,
yet steadily disappear.

To live in this skin,
Is to pass along burden to my offspring,
Is to teach them to love their shade
Is to have to teach them to love their shade
Is to prepare them for war over loving their shade.

To live in this skin,
Is to see bodies break like branches,
Is to see whole forests chopped down out of fear of their growth
Out of concern of their seeds spreading
Out of hope that their roots aren't grounded.

Tim Hall

To live in my skin,
Is to know my roots are grounded in the soil, rich
from the blood of my ancestors,
Is to know the families that came before me nourish my tree,
Is to see their shade in my bark
Their blood in my sap
Their tears in my leaves
Only, to be reminded of the lakes formed from their crying
when I see leaves at the feet of trees in autumn.

To live in my skin is to keep standing,
even when the trees around me are chopped to pieces,
Is to know my seeds can't be wiped out of existence,
Is to plant my roots in bloodied soil
Is to believe my tears aren't shed in vain
That my leaves shouldn't have to fall in constant mourning
That my life matters.

To live in my skin is to grow,
Even when the world around me walks past my pile of leaves,
Staring at its beautiful colors,
Not realizing they, are the reason my leaves fall.

Tim Hall is an educator, artist, and entrepreneur, from Detroit, MI. He began playing music at the age of 10, and found poetry in college as a way to share his thoughts on paper. Tim Hall draws inspiration from his lived experiences, charting the nuances of blackness, masculinity, and the beauties of life. Currently, Tim works at Berklee College of Music in Boston, MA and is a member of the Society of Urban Poetry.

The Black Handkerchief
(Ayotinapa)

Because I did not have
the power of a corrupt government behind me –
Or the farce of a cowardly media
that failed to speak the truth on my behalf.
Because they had threatened me at gun point
thinking it would be enough
to guarantee my silence.

Or because so many had disappeared already
that I would be too scared
to raise my voice.
But today I realized –
"What else could you do to me
that you haven't done already?"
The mothers in Juarez cry out for their
murdered daughters
and the ghosts of the battered men
haunt the very bridge that you hung them from.
What else can you do to me?
You took everything from me
and that was your biggest mistake
because you also took my fear.
And now, I am no longer afraid …

If I don't speak up now
I have only myself to blame
when the police come pounding at my door.
Are those their very trucks approaching?

Victor Avila

This simple piece of square cloth once insignificant –
now stands for more.
This black handkerchief is now my symbol of resistance.
I wave it in the face of those cowards who took the 43.
I lift it high in my angry fist waving it, waving it
And I will no longer use to wipe away my tears,
or the tears of my brothers and sisters.

It is my banner of defiance in the face of overwhelming odds.
It lets the world know I am not defeated,
that Mexico is not defeated …
And that we will bring the 43 home.

Victor Avila is an award-winning poet. Recent work has appeared the anthologies *Poetry of Resistance – Voices for Social Justice* and *The Border Crossed Us.* Victor has taught in California public schools for over twenty-five years.

CORTEZ CONTINUES

The colonial conquest is upon us,
The extermination of our races continues,
Still they build their missions to convert us,
Still they build their churches on top of our temples,
Still our skins are tattooed with a number that
Promises social security under the false
Worshipping of money,
Still war propaganda attempts to make enemies of brothers and sisters
And still, we believe.
Still we lay down and inhale the poison gas.
If history teaches us something is that the truth
About mass exterminations is always swept under sick blankets,
Under debris of professionally executed explosions,
And always under the name of God.

Juan Cárdenas is the Vice President of the Los Angeles Poet Society, a Non-Profit Community Organization, which serves to build a bridge between LA's creative communities, and also hosts and sponsors literary events in Southern California. Juan has been a part of California Poets in the Schools for 3 years, teaching at Beyond Baroque in the City of Venice and at Tia Chucha's Centro Cultural and Bookstore, inaugurated by Poet Luis J. Rodriguez, Los Angeles' current Poet Laureate. Juan is a classically trained Flautist with over 15 years' performance in Orchestras, and in Blues & Jazz ensembles. Juan fuses poetry and music in both his performances and lessons, and is now teaching the Ekphrastic Poetry method to our youth and elders.

Juan Cárdenas

Social Justice

Rubber bullets missed us
Flew by our faces
White, Black and Asian
Sometimes we're all equal
In the face of a riot
In the face of a class war
Debt shrapnel flying
Still some got an advantage
That's kind of hard to handle
When you're the color of the oppressor
Ego calling out "Scandal!"
I heard it said once
In the midst of fist pumps
That if life was a video game
Then being White was like playing
on easy mode, or rather cheat mode
Think about the metaphor
What about being a woman,
Or a color, or in natural form,
The decks stacked, Jack,
The banks backed
This system from its inception
The crown never unpacked
Who runs us
Turns our true selves from us
Turns our eyes closed, mouths closed
Outfoxed and tries to dumb us
Down to straight gun us
Would kill us for our stunners
The dead walk among us

Chris Devcich

Turned us all into gun nuts
So guns is the answer for a free radical state
As long as your color's clean, you can occupy – they'll wait
And in the meantime
Fiends die and we try to deny
That we ain't still human and these lies we will defy
Decry the obvious ugliness imprinted on us
Wand brush, skip a stone, a cross an emblem of the crushed,
Different lives matter more than those forced on slave ships
What you willing to sacrifice to balance out your status
Status quo: Nothing, not even what I can afford
'Cause all these Black Lives Matter is something I chose to ignore,
By carrying out my God given rights, as an American, It's my privilege
Don't try to tell me what I can do, Go back to your homeland! "Kiss this!"
But the Mayflower never left, nor the Nina, nor the Pinta,
Santa Maria sinking, see ya at the height of your corporate thinking,
History books been written by the victors and the – SHHHHHH!, Listen …
Some of those that burned crosses were the same that launched warships,
So worship everything that means nothing: Capitalism
In its late stage is so lame, but man who am I kidding,
This the way it's always been,
From the cradle to the plantation,
In America, we got too much to lose
To stare into what we're facing.

We Got Cops Killing Kids of Color Constantly

We got cops killing kids of color constantly
With impunity
Can't you see
When a man screams "I Can't Breathe!"?
Apparently not ...
All you wanna do is drop him
What happens when The People wanna start dropping cops?
What happens when the other shoe drops,
Or better yet the Molotov?
I'm not saying that's where my hearts trying to mob
I'm just saying that I can corrob-
orate, and be compassionate
To a whole generation who's insides are filled with fiery flames
Makes sense
Because the macro is the micro
And the world's on fire
So how about we fire the cops?
Before The People start
Firing on the cops
We can do this peaceful
Or we can do this just like the beast do
I pray that more don't have to die
And their lives are erased under oath of a lie
From a cop but really he's a man
Underneath it all

Chris Devcich

And the way he treats those he kills and brutalizes
Illustrates he sees himself small
Swallowed by the system alive
Spit out as a robot
Rottin' empty inside
Take a look in the mirror
Stare into your own eyes
I'm doing it as I write now –
All of humanity's inside.

Chris Devcich is a musician, songwriter, emcee, poet, DJ, producer, filmmaker and activist, to name a few hats he wears. He is a Hip Hop artist who performs under the alias Guido Corleone and a member of the Venice, Los Angeles-based Hip Hop crew the Luminaries. But perhaps more than anything – he is trying to be a helper. His Mother was born and raised in the St. Louis area, growing up in the town of Kirkwood, MO, which has brought him to St. Louis many times throughout his life. Having traveled and toured across the country and various parts of the world, alongside artists ranging from the likes of Dead Prez to the Dead Kennedys. Devcich loves rocking shows, connecting with People from all over and learning from their Culture. In embracing his own humanness, and channeling it through his art, he is finding a way to see all things – and all life – as relative. He shines a light into his own darkness to reveal The Truth, standing with The People in Love and Solidarity.

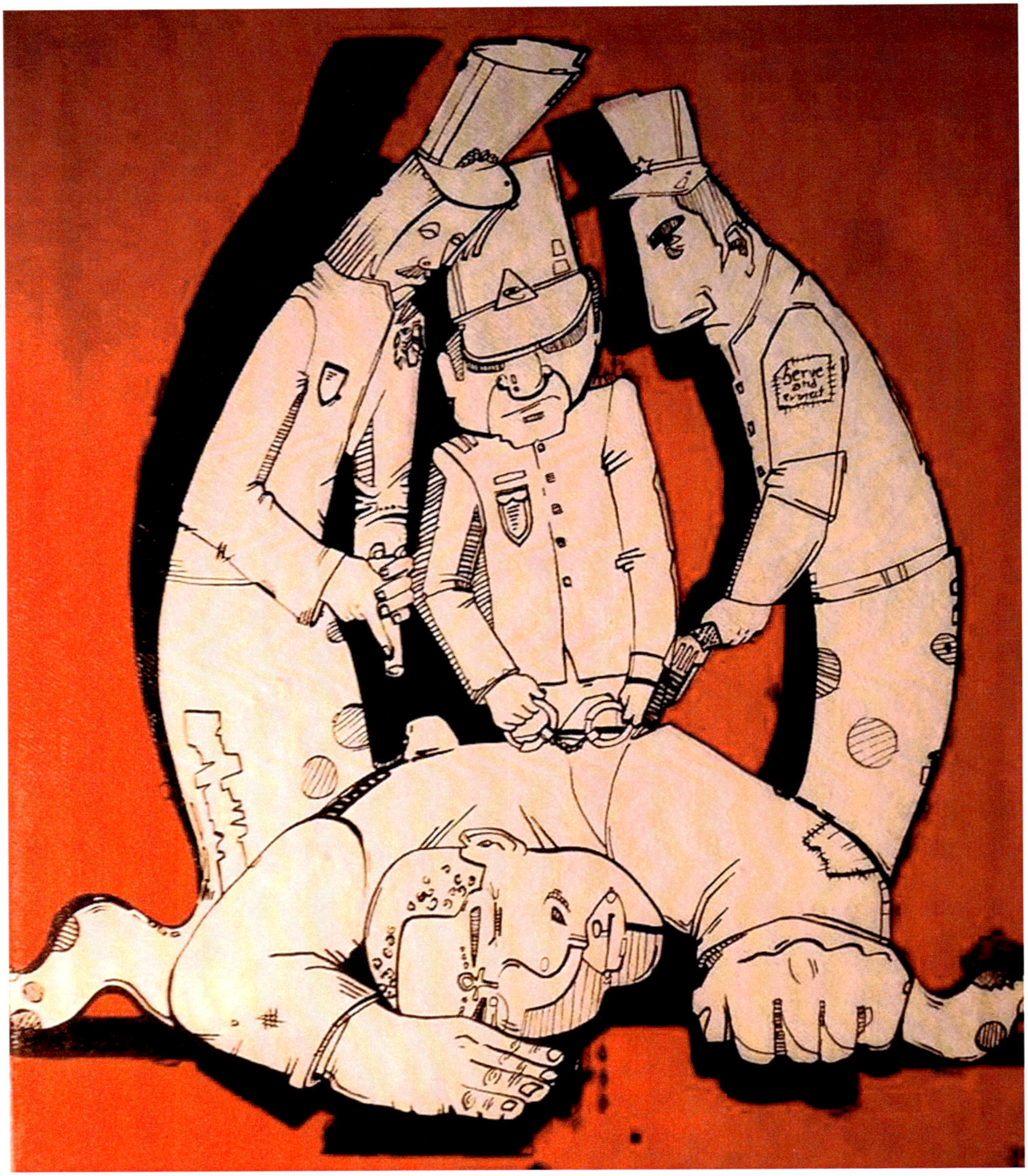

BREATH

On the ground, Eric panted, "I can't breathe."
Sandra is stopped for not signaling and she can't leave.

In Ferguson, black bodies lay on the ground.
Does someone check to see if a breath can be found?

I watch the news and I can't breathe ... well.
Who has sold their souls to Mephistopheles?

A black teenage boy was shot in a park
by police in broad daylight. His breath,

he was still breathing for a while
'til the light dimmed and dimmed until

it became dark. And the blood pooled
and his sister who ran towards his dying body

laid in handcuffs on the ground.
Not knowing what was going on.

While the good lay beneath the earth,
The murderers are set free —

breathing, breathing ... they are breathing
But I can't breathe.

Teresa Mei Chuc is author of *Red Thread* (Fithian Press, 2012) and *Keeper of the Winds* (FootHills Publishing, 2014), She was born in Saigon, Vietnam and immigrated to the U.S. under political asylum with her mother and brother shortly after the Vietnam War while her father remained in a Vietcong "reeducation" camp for nine years. Her poetry appears in journals such as *CONSEQUENCE Magazine, EarthSpeak Magazine, Hawai'i Pacific Review, Kyoto Journal, The Prose-Poem Project, The National Poetry Review, Rattle, Verse Daily* and in anthologies such as *New Poets of the American West* (Many Voices Press, 2010), *With Our Eyes Wide Open: Poems of the New American Century* (West End Press, 2014), and *Mo' Joe* (Beatlick Press, 2014).

Teresa Mei Chuc

Double Kwansaba* after Michael Brown

When police are the threat, who's there
to protect? When walking in the street
can get you busted, shot, or beat
just for being black, talking back, looking
wrong, or looking strong – how can we
really be: a viable city, where people
can live in harmony? a free country?

With tanks in the street, who or
what do they defeat? No good results,
only bad; fear is what drives us
mad. And fear, the root of hate,
becomes the Police State. Instead of tear
gas, hear us! Let's relate, for a
start, human to human, heart to heart.

A Kwansaba is a form invented by Eugene B. Redmond: seven lines, seven words per line, no more than seven letters per word.

Michael Castro

Report from the Streets around St. Louis

Trolls patrolling the bridges & byways
out of town,
highwaymen, stagecoach robbers, thuggees,
all waylaying travelers, taking their money,
high-jacking the strongbox, sometimes
leaving people dead lying on the ground.
Historical images abound
of thieves & cutthroats on the road.

Here & now,
the police play that role.
Things are the same, but different.

Trolls of old did not discriminate,
targeting wealth in motion
whatever its complexion.
They operated outside the law,
as enemies of the State.

Today's trolls in blue
represent the State,
cruise in white patrol cars,
like a squadron of Lone Rangers riding Silver,
heroes in their own mind movie,
the Law at their command.

Michael Castro

Unlike historical models,
they discriminate
carefully,
profiling, targeting
not the rich, but
poor people with the wrong shade of skin,
those they are charged
with protecting & serving.

Heavily armed
against the citizenry
with citations & bullets,
patrolling neighborhoods
like an occupying army,
backed by military hardware,
inclined by job stress & training
to escalate at hints of weary objection
or resistance,
to shoot to kill if panicked
by real or imagined threat,
they serve City Hall's
racist & classist biases,
& a voracious appetite for cash.

Victims who miss hearings
or can't pay through the nose
are served & protected
with arrest warrants,
do time in modern debtors prisons
for broken taillights,
illegal turns, failure to signal
and the like.
Jailed for lack of money.

Who can serve & protect the family
while in jail?
Who can go to work
while in jail?
Who can pay the bills
while in jail?

And who can do a damn thing
lying dead in a cell or in the street?

Ask Sandra Bland, Corey Jones,
Tamir Rice, Eric Garner, Michael Brown.
Ask so many others, tragically & needlessly
cut down. Ask the decades. Ask the historical record.

And so I must insist
BLACK LIVES MATTER
to those with dimes on their eyes
instead of Justice's blindfolds,
to those armed with hair trigger tempers & the Law,
to those with weapons of disruption
on pads in their pockets,
& weapons of destruction on their hips,
to governments exploiting & terrorizing
their own citizens,
and to all those who, with comfortable opinions,
deny full humanity to another,
not knowing they deny their own:

BLACK LIVES MATTER.

And to those who mask denial
with smug self-approval
with the counter, "All lives matter,"
I say,
Too many unnecessary deaths speak loud.
Too many harassments, citations, arrests;
Too many fines, too many compound charges;
Too many days & nights in jails;
Too much stress; Too much suffering;
Too many, too many deaths –
drown out & expose that lame retort.

BLACK LIVES MATTER:
It must be printed in capital letters.
It must be shouted.

BLACK LIVES MATTER.

Don't fear it, hear it.
Embrace it.
Things must change.

Michael Castro is a poet, translator, arts activist and educator. Castro is co-founder of the literary organization and magazine River Styx and hosted the Poetry Beat radio show for fifteen years. He has been named one of St. Louis's top fifty writers by the Missouri History Museum, has received the Guardian Angel of St. Louis Poetry Award from River Styx, and been named a Warrior Poet by Word in Motion, all for lifetime achievement. The *St. Louis Post Dispatch* has called him "a legend in St. Louis Poetry." In 2015 he was named the first Poet Laureate of St. Louis.

SANDTOWN, HOME OF FREDDIE GRAY

Sandtown
In Baltimore
Abandoned houses
Littered streets
High rates of lead poisoning
Among children
Children who have no Little League
Children who play
Or try to play
In the streets
Before cops pick them up
For playing in the streets
Children who grow into Freddie Gray
Old enough to be thrown
Into the back of a police wagon
To lie in handcuffs
And shackles
With no seat belt
For what cops call
A "rough ride
A penny ride, a nickel ride
A cowboy ride
Common practice
For cops needing
A little entertainment
Police car lynching

Of young black men
Riding in police vans
Freddie Gray
Broken spine
Murdered
By police
The protectors of the people
Given the common rough treatment
Thousands of others have been given
For the crime
Of walking on the streets
Of Sandtown
Baltimore
And running from police
Knowing the police
Can murder
Citizens
Like Freddie Gray
Can lynch
Citizens
Like Freddie Gray
With a simple
"Rough ride"
In the back
Of a police van

Karen Melander-Magoon

SHADOW

There is a shadow on the horizon
The arm of injustice and deception
Spreads a great dark shadow
We carry candles only
To lighten the dark
To shine for emancipation
Voting rights open internet free speech
End to mass incarceration death penalty
Stigmatization born by children for lifetimes
Incarcerated once for being black
Or poor
We carry candles
But there is not enough light
Jim Crow still lurks in the darkness
Jim Crow still sabotages minorities
Sabotages free speech and voting rights
With gerrymandering profiling murder
Corporate-backed surveillance
While Islam State murders children
For being educated
We murder children
Or the poor
For being poor
For being black
For being unable
To afford an education
For walking in the streets
Unarmed
For walking down stairs
Unarmed

Karen Melander-Magoon

For selling cigarettes
To pay the bills
Unarmed
Only 11,501 allegations
Against city police officers in New York
Were filed in 2013
Only
Only 7% increase in complaints in 2014
Only
Ironic that police officers
Hired to protect civilians
Are trained in Israel
To treat civilians
As enemies
Where is the power
Of law?
Where is the power
Of the First and Fourth
Amendments
To our sacred
Constitution?
Where is light
Sufficient to erase
The dark shadow
Of injustice?

Karen Melander-Magoon, D.Min., holds a Bachelors Degree in Music from Indiana University, sang major roles in opera for nearly two decades in Europe and has composed four one-woman musical portraits of historical figures, including Clara Barton, Georgia O'Keeffe, Lillie Langtry, and the French poet, Colette. She has also written a sung history of Hawaii, called "Ohana" and a staged monologue called, Eve II with some vocal interludes, telling the story of the myths from a female perspective. She is listed in the European Publishers VIP Who is Who. Karen has a Masters in Counseling from Boston University, a Master of Divinity equivalency through the Graduate Theological Union, as well as her Doctor of Ministry from San Francisco Theological Seminary.

90

SAY HER NAME

my sisters have strewn their bodies across the pavement

breath taken under moonlight

lament the way her skin blends into the night

you will forget her

the way she moved across daylight

a Queen shining from the inside

say her name

repeat her memory until it becomes the echo of her laughter

ignite the candles to remember our fallen daughters

pursed lips and clenched fists hold onto her

keep her safe in the ever after

for those will come who question her character

the reasons why it was and is ok to silence her

say her name

black women's lives matter

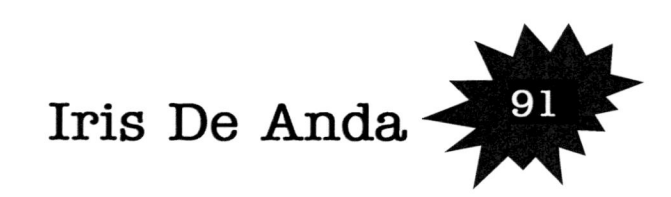

Iris De Anda

this american night is too dark to swallow

it is the colliding of history and those who quit listening to the master

sing her songs of freedom

she was humming the chants since birth

now we must shout until we are heard

say her name

Sandra Bland

Tanisha Anderson

Rekia Boyd

Miriam Carey

Alexia Christian

Michelle Cusseaux

Shelly Frey

Mya Hall

Meagan Hockaday

Kayla Moore

say her name say her name say her name

SOME SAY *for Trayvon Martin*

Somewhere a mother
weeps blood
over daughters & sons
under the night sky
stars reflect
the fallen ones

Somehow a man
blindly walks
over history repeating
under cover of self defense
hearts break
no justice beating

Sometimes a human
seeks one truth
over generations of pain
under the gray clouds
echoes drifting
the tainted rain

Someone a boy
flies free
over unjust juries
under the flag
candles burn
the people's fury

Iris De Anda is a writer, activist, and practitioner of the healing arts. A womyn of color of Mexican and Salvadorean descent. A native of Los Angeles she believes in the power of spoken word, poetry, storytelling, and dreams. She has been published in Mujeres de Maiz Zine, Loudmouth Zine: Cal State LA, OCCUPY SF poems from the movement, Revolutionary Poets Brigade Los Angeles Anthology, Seeds of Resistance, In the Words of Women, Twenty: In Memoriam and online at La Bloga. She is an active contributor to Poets Responding to SB 1070. She performs at community venues and events throughout the Los Angeles area & Southern California. She hosted The Writers Underground Open Mic 2012 at Mazatlan Theatre and 100,000 Poets for Change 2012, 2013, and 2014 at the Eastside Cafe. She currently hosts The Writers Underground Open Mic every Third Thursday of the month at the Eastside Cafe. Author of CODESWITCH: Fires from Mi Corazon. www.irisdeanda.com

BRUTALITY GAMES❖

Chorus: Santa Rosa California
Andy Lopez   from Santa Rosa
Andy Lopez   from California.

City fog entwines our glance with a last cry
The fate of a child enrages
my tongue to conjuring words
A 13-year-old child's heart
a seed   trampled on the street

My hands open like an umbrella to shield his life
from lead rain that bullets   over the inner city

A child's dream of life reduced to a graveyard
13-year-old holding a toy gun
hits concrete under a bully's downpour
His life crushed alongside asphalt
                                          The killer
rinses honor on impunity decrees
while this child's hope for justice
darts on comatose rainbows

Chorus: Santa Rosa California
Andy Lopez   from Santa Rosa
Andy Lopez   from California.

❖ Santa Rosa, California, October 22, 2013 the 13-year-old Andy Lopez was carrying a toy gun. Sheriff Erick Gelhaus (an Iraq war veteran and a firearms instructor) that spotted Lopez at 3:14 pm approached him from behind and opened fire. 17 seconds. Gelhaus fired eight shots at Lopez. Seven bullets hit Andy within six seconds. One round hit Lopez on his side while he was turning to face police, according to an autopsy. At 3:14:17 pm, after the shooting, the cops handcuffed Lopez. No charges would be filed against the cop. 1,206 people were killed by police brutality from January 2014 to January 2015.

Antonieta Villamil

"La poesía es un arma cargada de futuro"
~ Gabriel Celaya

SONG FOR THE WORKER WOMAN

It is happening right now in my heart, in my mind, on a city street of any country; but I need to take that the revolution is not here because conformity is sitting its big potato ass on a couch of misled-me tales and we, the outraged 99% have to push all at once with all power from the ground up but first, need to dig that we are the base. Here I break the screen before the system implodes a replay in my face. Here I exercise the muscle of rights before they become flaccid but first, I need to digest this: I protest, YES, because the nipple finds its way to the needy mouth but I watch what kind of lollypop I get to shut me up. Administered like Prozac, the revolution is bipolar, sold to people as genetically altered mad cow with scorpion genes and beware, smells like mass destruction.

The revolution is at home, teaching children another way; teaching that public woman means leader and not prostitute, as it is written in the dictionary of men, and while you grasp that, take this: Organized women of the world will close the legs not to give war more kids, still attached to placentas as body bags. These are "weapons charged with future" and take these words to heart; the revolution is a planet of hungry widows with no work; homeless women and children with a future against all common sense. And what is for breakfast and dinner is next war until the next war of poor against poor, while the 1% predator kind, breaks a richer laugh.

Antonieta Villamil is an international award winning bilingual poet, writer, singer and editor with over 11 published books. She focuses her writing on the forgotten ones and honors them with a persistence that compels us to hear their voices. She directs the review and salon *Poesía Féstival* that brings poetry to the underserved community of native Spanish speakers in Los Angeles. antonietavillamil.blogspot.com

Antonieta Villamil

An Amendment in Angst

Freedom of speech held at gunpoint by your right to bear arms,
Religious freedom obliterated by your groundless wars,
Medical care denied by your greed,
Advances in science kept at bay by your fear of the unknown,
Free spirits caged by your laws,
Frame me
Cuff me
Chain me
Lock me up
Shoot me
Kill me
I'm just dying to fight for the future.

S.L. Kerns

Gun at My Head

I'd pray for you,
Except...

My words are held against me in a court of law.
Forced to bite my tongue as you shout racial slurs,
My hands cuffed behind me as I am brutalized.
A gun at my head,
I am only freed when it's time to take an oath on a religious book of your choosing.

I'd pray for you,
Except...

S.L. Kerns may have southern roots, but he has branched out to a life in Asia. He spent 5 years lost in Bangkok before moving to his current home in Japan. He loves soaking in words of wisdom, and trains both mind and body. He teaches English and has recently begun writing, using his surplus of wild experiences to fuel his works. His work had been published or is forthcoming in *Flash Fiction Magazine, 101 Words*, and *47-16: A Collection of Poetry and Fiction Inspired by David Bowie*. He also blogs for Muay Thai Lab.

GUARDIAN ANGELS?

a pistol is held to your forehead
in a bosky alley of the night

you search for the face behind the hand
as you wait for the click of the trigger
and

instead you see
the hand holding the gun pull back

you take a deep breath
and when your lungs
fill up with the air of hope
a blow hits your temple

a stick-up
the thought enters you
together with the pain

two men stand above you
kick your face
your groin
repeatedly
without rushing

one of them leans above you

"you little piece of crap
be happy
you still
alive"

perspiring at you

Gabor Gyukics (b. 1958) Hungarian-American poet, literary translator is the author of 7 books of original poetry, 4 in Hungarian, 2 in English, 1 in Bulgarian and 11 books of translations including *A Transparent Lion*, selected poetry of Attila József and an anthology of North American Indigenous poets in Hungarian. His latest book titled *a hermit has no plural* was published by Singing Bone Press in the fall of 2015. His poetic works and translations have been published in over 200 magazines and anthologies in English, Hungarian and other languages worldwide. He received the Füst Milan translator's prize in 1999, the National Cultural Foundation grant in 2007, the 2012 Salvatore Quasimodo special prize for poetry and the Poesis 25 Prize for Poetry in Satu Mare, Romania in 2015. Thanks to a CEC Arts Link grant he established the first Open Mike and Jazz Poetry reading series in Hungary in 1999. He is a member of the Belletrist Association of Hungary and the Hungarian Translators Association.

Gabor Gyukics

Thoughts on Swallowing a Butterfly

Butterflies,
such a fragile incarnation
of what went before.
Warriors, according to the Mayans,
dead warriors ready
to be transformed,
transformed into butterflies.
Butterflies,
surely too fragile
to make warriors,
too easily destroyed
in their new metamorphosis.
But they can wait
for their next transformation
So take care if you swallow a butterfly.
Butterflies,
vigorous egg layers
that can reproduce themselves,
warriors,
mutating again to find
new ways to fight back,
to invade the invaders,
enslave the enslavers,
exploit
the new possibilities.
So take care if you swallow a butterfly.
And I can wait.
I have been waiting a long time
to see Henry Kissinger choke
on a butterfly.
I can wait.
Perhaps there's still hope
that the butterflies
will worm their way inside
and destroy them all.
I can wait.
So take care if you swallow a butterfly.

Lynn White lives in north Wales. Her work is influenced by issues of social justice and events, places and people she has known or imagined. She is especially interested in exploring the boundaries of dream, fantasy and reality. Her poem 'A Rose for Gaza' was shortlisted for the Theatre Cloud 'War Poetry for Today' competition 2014 and has since appeared in several journals and anthologies. Poems have also recently been included in anthologies which include – Harbinger Asylum's 'To Hold a Moment Still', Stacey Savage's 'We Are Poetry, an Anthology of Love Poems', Community Arts Ink's 'Reclaiming Our Voices', 'The Border Crossed Us' by VAGABOND, 'Civilised Beasts' from Weasel Press, 'Alice In Wonderland' by Silver Birch Press and a number of on-line and print journals.

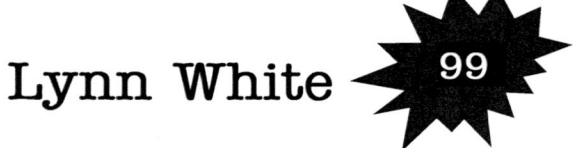

Lynn White

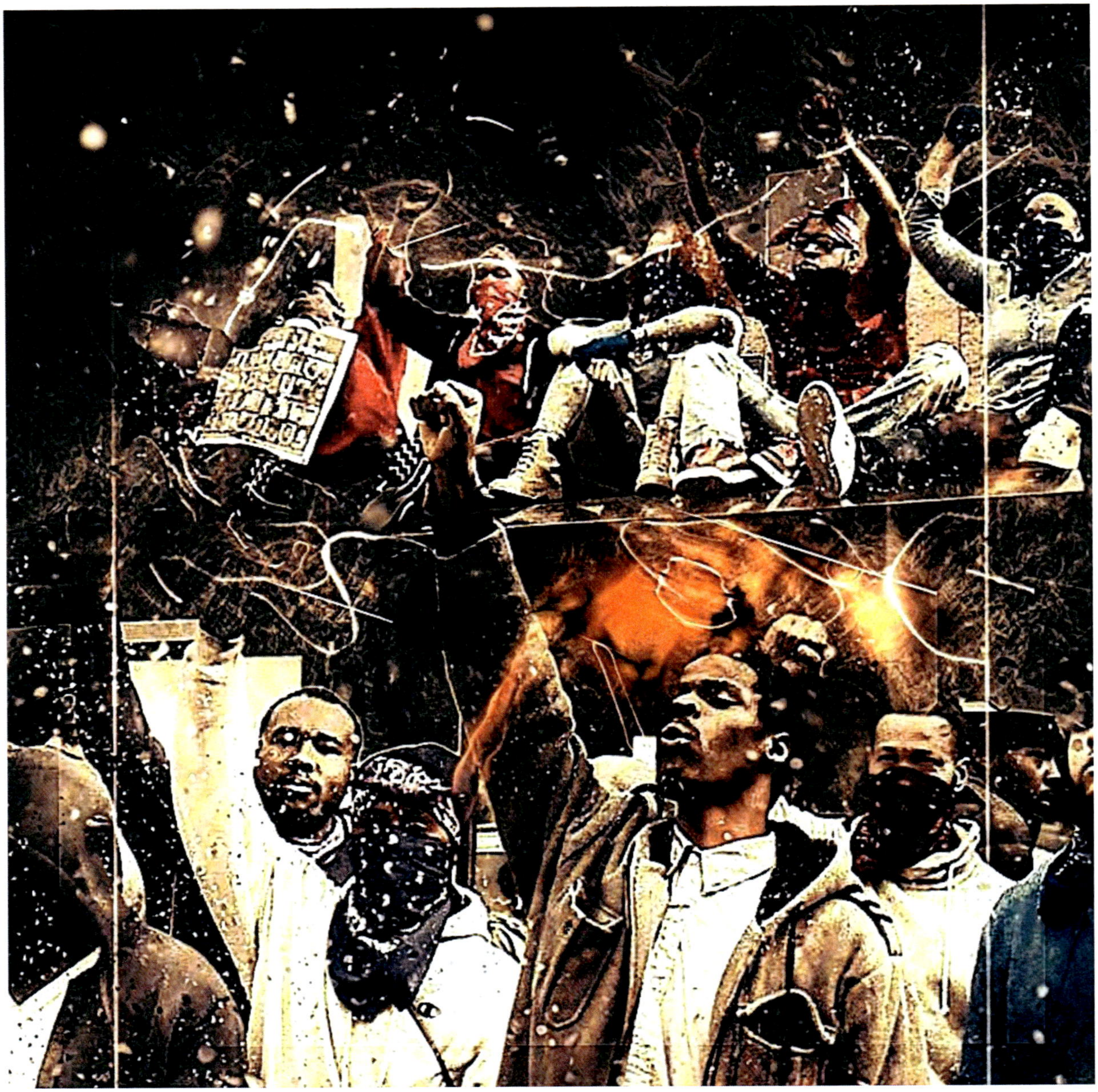

Poem for a New Dream

In the aftermath of the Pulse nightclub massacre, Orlando, Florida, June 12, 2016

Hate becomes death becomes hate.
The world unravels in fear.

Columbine: 13 students and a teacher gone.
Sandy Hook: 20 children and 6 adults murdered.
Charleston, North Carolina: 9 black churchgoers killed.
San Bernardino: 14 men and women destroyed.
Orlando, Florida: 50 patrons of a LGBTQ nightclub slaughtered.

Hate that shouts without a voice,
that uses bullets to speak,
that has a finality to its grief,
that can't see because this rage has no eyes…

No brain.
No heart.
No connections.

Hate in Wounded Knee, 1890: 300 Native men, women, children wiped out.

Ludlow, Colorado, 1914: National Guard and John D. Rockefeller's company guards kill some 25 men, women, and children during coal miners' strike.

Tulsa Oklahoma, 1921: Upwards of 300 black residents slaughtered by whites
In 1919 alone, hundreds killed in more than 300 riots against blacks.

Some 4,000 blacks lynched from 1860 to 1950.
Around 700 Mexicans in roughly the same years.
Millions erased bringing Africans to America….

In the first 15 years of the 21st century, police killed unarmed black residents in Ferguson, Baltimore, Oakland, New York, Los Angeles…

Luis J. Rodriguez

Salinas police killed 5 unarmed Mexican and Salvadoran farm workers in 2014.

Black lives matter because when they stop being killed, we're all free.

Hate against the raped women (1 in 5 women raped in the United States), killing women's choices for their bodies, killing and killing and killing.

Oklahoma City: 168 blown to pieces.
Twin Towers, New York: 2,752 massacred.

6 millions Jews destroyed in the Holocaust.

When right becomes hate, it loses its right.

When walls are the response
—or invasions, drone attacks, torture, perpetual war…

Hate rules.

Ask Hitler. Ask Mussolini. Ask Pinochet.

Ask the 75,000 killed during the 1980s in El Salvador,
or 100,000 Mayan villagers in Guatemala,
or the hundreds of protesting students in Tlatelolco, Mexico.

Remember Ayotzinapa.

90 percent of Native peoples dead within 50 years of European invasion.
I recall Malcolm teaching that in the ghetto we're seeing "the hate that hate produced."

I've seen this in the barrio.
In the reservation.
In the trailer park.

Self-hate is also hate.
It's in suicides of LGBTQ youth hounded to death.

When an interviewer insinuated to Muhammad Ali
that he learned to hate white people
from being a Muslim, Ali said, "I learned to hate white people from white people."

When Gays and Trans folk get beaten, stabbed, shot, just for being what they
can't help but be, hate is the normality of our existence,
the fabric in our tapestry, the fetid air we breathe.

White. Black. Brown. Women. Men.

Dead.

Christians. Buddhists. Muslims. Hindu. Natives. Nonbelievers.

Dead.

And transitional beings.

Dead.

More than 200,000 annihilated in Hiroshima and Nagasaki.

Hate is in the blood.

Guns don't hate. But those who want guns in all our hands do.

When 6,800 people died since 1998 trying to cross the Mexico-U.S. border.
And 164,000 killed, with 30,000 missing, since 2006 in Mexican drug wars.

When hate says we can't reach out across all walls, then tear down those walls.

Poverty is hate. Prison is hate. Families without homes…

Hate. Hate. Hate.

When Martin Luther King, Jr. got assassinated
—and John F. Kennedy, Medgar Evers, Malcolm X, Robert Kennedy,
Ruben Salazar, Rudy Lozano, Harvey Milk, John Lennon…

Hate sang its sanguine song.

When 15,000 young people in the barrios and ghettos of Los Angeles died from gang violence from 1980 to 2000.

When Chicago sees hundreds of mostly black and brown youth destroyed every year for forty years.

When the murder capitals of the world are Detroit, New Orleans, San Pedro Sula, Ciudad Juarez, Johannesburg… hate capitalizes.

When refugees of hate now have Syrian faces, Afghani faces, Iraqi faces, Honduran faces, poor faces…

That's hate. Self hate. The hate that hate produced.

Hate is an industry. Hate makes some people rich. Capitalism is hate.

No heart.
No connections.
No brain.
No eyes.

The answer to hate is not hate. Justified by hateful Gods in people's minds.

When even love is a reason to be killed, then hate is the heart gone mad.

As prayers shroud the dead, guns sales rise,
and defense budgets take up the majority of our tax dollars
(even if most days we forget we're at war).

Violence sells movies, books, music.
And the violent, victims and perpetrators alike,
fills jails and mental institutions.
When in every poor neighborhood you can buy guns and drugs all you want, but you can't buy a book?

We need people to be Queer. Unique. Different. To make us more human.

When access to love, peace, connections, hearts, brains,
and books becomes revolutionary.

Then revolution is the only way to go. An armed revolution, yes,
but not of guns.

Armed with art, connections, hearts, brains, books,
and a multiplicity of imaginations.

Imagine… imagine… imagine.

We reweave the unraveling cloth of our lives with dreams, not screams.

Without hate.
Without violence.
Without fear.

So love becomes life becomes love.

Luis J. Rodriguez is the Poet Laureate of Los Angeles, appointed by Mayor Eric Garcetti in the fall of 2014. He has 15 published books in poetry, children's literature, short stories, the novel, memoirs, and nonfiction. He's best known for the 1993 memoir "Always Running, La Vida Loca, Gang Days in L.A." now close to half a million copies sold. He is also founding editor of the renown cross-cultural press, Tia Chucha Press, now in its 25th year, and co-founder/president of Tia Chucha's Centro Cultural & Bookstores. He travels throughout the United States speaking at schools, colleges, universities, conferences, prisons, juvenile lockups, homeless shelters, migrant camps, Native American reservations, libraries, and more. He has also done talks, readings, workshops, and reporting in Mexico, Canada, El Salvador, Guatemala, Nicaragua, Honduras, Puerto Rico, Venezuela, Peru, Argentina, Japan, England, France, Holland, Austria, Italy, Germany, and Bosnia-Herzegovina. Luis' work has been published in publications like the New York Times, Los Angeles Times, Chicago Tribune, L.A. Weekly, U.S. News & World Report, San Jose Mercury, Philadelphia Inquirer magazine, The Nation, Grand Street, The Guardian, Christian Science Monitor, Fox News Latino, and Huffington Post, among others. For more information: www.luisjrodriguez.com.

SLAVES NO MORE

A Tribute to Trayvon Martin and the "Others"

*"Oh, freedom, Oh, freedom over me.
Before I'd be a slave, I'd be buried in my grave. . ."* ~ Negroes Spiritual

Our humanity is in our DNA
Our dignity tossed overboard by the meat ships that sailed the Atlantic
"No more weeping and a wailing. . ." freedom physically for us has arrived.
Our suffering now is of an intellectual and spiritual kind.

What would Nat Turner, who led rebellion in 1839,
say to our black young folks today?
"Your freedom came at a very high cost,
but some yawl still choosing to be lost!
We still live like we're not oppressed in a land;
marginalized by bad water and police brutality.
The shackles on our mind is slavery; the overseer, mass communications

Steals the soul and exploits our Nubian minds,
sells our souls up the rivers of destructive imaging.
Dresses up and pants down is an indication
that our self-esteem ground level thinking.
Black men stop generically stop labeling black women hoes,
the commodity of capitalism that is not the true meaning of Hip Hop.

Our cognitive pathology leads us to our death;
living without any rest from racial, institutional, psychological warfare.
Our condition has improved some,
but too many of our children are dying by the gun.
No longer, do we hear the beat of our mother's homeland drums.
Run, tum, tum, tum, from the enemy, stand strong,
rum, tum, tum, tum, and he will flee.

Dawnna "Ashay" Mathieu

It's drowned out with the rhetoric of political hatred,
evil schemes, and death of reality.
Our great accomplishments are ignored,
morality's miscarried that baby of hedonism.
Our President Obama's image is shared on the internet
with a noose around his neck.
All hands on deck, for the public lynching of racial equality
and justice on Fox news.

A shameful sight, brought aboard the ship Cora,
still not adored even as the leader of the land.
Our salute to the souls that were lost across the Atlantic,
a moment of silence please.
Our salute to the souls that survived the daily,
horror of rejection, by racial molestation.
Our Nation's Congress publically dishonors our Pontus, hoots, hollers and
hackles during his Public Address, no one get upset, but let it happen to
Donald Trump, and the loud mouth idiot is escorted out.
They will stand up for their own.

The gales from the post side of Hell is the ship we came on, now that we're here
generations will revere or claim to, this great Nation. History concurs, no
blacks, no America, no *National* sound in music.

This post-colonial travesty of justice; witnessed in the Trayvon Martin case is
testimony there's still work to do, for our freedom, saying otherwise is denial to
me. . .

Martin Luther King said, "Let freedom ring. . ."
In the 21st century the bells of freedom have not stop tolling.
"Let freedom ring. . ." for, Trayvon Martin. . . for Flint Michigan. . .
"Let freedom ring. . ." for, injustice in America,
"Let freedom ring. . ." for, you for me.

Freedom will ring, we will continue to sing songs that uplift and inspire
The same loud cry that our ancestors shouted, slaves, no more.
Slaves no, more too racial injustice; we focus on our healing.
We can conquer the demons of past traumatic slave disorder.

Our strength is in the memory of Shirley Chisolm, Mary McCloud Bethune, and W.E.B. Dubois, Thurgood Marshall and others. Our economic advantage is recorded in the memory of the Montgomery Bus Boycott.

This nation's dependence on our contributions to American society in all the areas of the arts stands conferred on the intellectual prowess and courage of our ancestors. Our dignity is in the sweat of their brow.

This nation: built on the backs of slaves is still great in the twenty-first century, our legacy continues.

Our desire for liberty is still the counter-narrative of liberation
in the new millennium. Understand our intention, we will continue to lead.

We will work until, The New Jim Crow in America stops dancing, on the toe of our brothers and sisters. Trying to put their lives back together.
Here us when we say, Slaves, no more.

Dawnna "Ashay" Mathieu: A major focus of Ashay's literary work is writing poetry and narratives reflecting the diversity of the African Diaspora experience. Her scholarly research investigates the lives and perils of the Second Diasporic experience of Black America during the late 19th and 20th centuries. Particularly, calling attention to black POWs, who were arrested and jailed in Nazi concentration camps and their African American liberators during WWII. Ashay's poetry writing is uniquely merited with the style of Ekphrastic technique commenting on other art forms (such as visual art and music) produced by Black Americans in Europe during the middle and late 1940s. *The Unveiling of the Obscured: Black Victims of the Holocaust* is a lecture and performance event that Ashay has created to highlight the life and work of two black Holocaust victims during WWII. Currently, Ashay is preparing her manuscript of poetry for publication with a small press.

HANDS OF THE CONVICT

The man is out of the picture, head cut off, body
so imprisoned all you see are his hands, wrists
and forearms resting on the crossbars.
One hand folds around the other as a kind of solace.
They droop as though they'd given up hope
but the jagged nails are dark with defiance
and the bulging veins show strength.
Those hands could be patiently waiting for
a legal messiah or illegal lover. Or they might
be pondering justice and incarceration
as they wait for redemption. Is the man
behind them a killer or rapist or just another
innocent swept up by racist cops? Is there blood
in his eyes, or tears? For all its artistry,
the photo doesn't say how long he's been there
or whether he's in solitary. All it tells
is that the hands are weary and that you'd try
to free them if you were close enough.
If you could break into prison and walk
through the clanging corridors and enter the cell,
then, maybe, you'd see the man.

Sherman Pearl is immediate past president of the Beyond Baroque Literary Arts Center in Venice and was a founding member of the Los Angeles Poetry Festival. He also was a director of the Valley Contemporary Poets and a co-editor of California Quarterly. His work is widely published and his most recent books are *The Poem in Time of War* and *Elegy for Myself.*

Edward Menefee, Murdered Inmate, Attica Prison Rebellion, September 13th, 1971

Maybe Mr. Menefee wasn't nice.
Maybe he wanted to kill somebody.

I've stolen. More than once I've wanted
to split a skull
for less than a boot to the ass.

Did he lift a 2x4 to face the charging cops?

Dude, that guy was hauling ass.
He didn't turn around at all.

The police made something up.

"He posed a deadly threat.
He swung a length of lumber at a trooper."

Let me drop some knowledge:

weeks later in the green light of ICU,
crying for his teddy bear, then his mom, he died.

Paul David Adkins

Alfred Williams, Murdered Inmate, Attica Prison Rebellion, September 13th, 1971

Double aught buckshot lifts the lid off my skull
quick as an inmate cook set to stir a kettle of creamed corn.

Even as I fall, I think, *Damn it!*

I think, *Lord Jesus!*

Because I can
still think,
for that last second, that last precious second-and-a-half.

All the way down, my thoughts are mine, even to the ground.

I do not waste them
on cops.

I am not afraid.

I am not.

I am

Paul David Adkins lives in New York and works as a counselor. Lit Riot Press published his debut poetry collection *La Doña, La Llorona* in May, 2016. Additionally, this publisher has dual-released his volumes *Flying over Baghdad with Sylvia Plath* and *Operational Terms and Graphics* in November, 2016.

Paul David Adkins

112

AUTHORITY REVISIONED

My brother wanted to be a cop
to change the system from the inside
He impressed them at interviews
but the rookie cop job always
went to a Republican with security experience
They suggested he consider social services
as another way to be a positive male role model
He got a job as a night watchman,
but the hours sucked and it was boring.
He's in India now, with his wife,
while she helps establish a Microsoft funded charter school.
They blog about raw sewage flooding the streets of Mumbai
in monsoon season, how it takes all day to buy milk, their encounter with leeches,
the impossibility of finding lettuce, how Starbucks is exactly the same.
Seattle area police have a reputation for brutal over reaction;
they need men like my brother, strong, creative, compassionate men
who can show children how to be powerful without being abusive.

I've never had a really bad experience with a cop
though seeing a patrol car still causes an attack of nerves,
inciting that primal fear of being accused of doing something wrong.
Most cops I've encountered are polite,
though my son has had two unpleasant experiences
involving bike safety. He was chastised for riding a bike
on the Square, and pulled over for making a rolling stop,
with threats that this could affect his ability to get a license.
Scare tactics make me sick. Two cops being overbearing jerks,
trying to scare my son into a "law-abiding" citizen.
Bullying by any other name. . .

Megan D. Robinson

A friend was tear gassed at a peaceful demonstration
in downtown Seattle. One of my poetry mentors,
Vicki Edmonds, was abused by her father, a cop.
She explores that dichotomy that he was supposed to be a good guy
but was a monster at home, in her work. She's a poet in the schools, using poetry
as a healing tool, working with Seattle area teens to use the processing power
of poetry to overcome their past experiences and find their voice.

My personal experience with brutality is more intimate.
He was supposed to be my best friend, my soul mate, my world king.
He labeled himself a feminist, which was an excuse to expect me
to liberate myself from the anchors of feminine anatomy and think like him.
All the verbal abuse was for my own good.
Brute force is not true power or authority.

Megan D Robinson. I'm a single mom with a love of words and a desire for justice. I think poetry can be a powerful tool for social change. I've been involved with a local spoken word group, Soapbox Speakeasy, and wrote Authority Revisioned, for a fundraiser we had for Black Lives Matter. Additionally, I'm a freelance writer, and have written for local and regional newspapers, as well as blogs and websites. My poetry chapbook, *No Longer An Ingenue,* won the 2014 Bluelight Press Poetry Prize. I've published poems in a handful of anthologies. I live in Iowa, with my teenage son and our supernaturally cute Pomeranian, Chewbacca.

BLACK & BLUE

I will go on living without
knowing if I would have survived
that December night
with my mother's skin
instead of my father's.
Stop resisting, he said.
I have seen the statistics;
they are not conclusory,
but they are alarming.
Watchmen find reasons to
reach for their arms.
Stop resisting, he said.

Our black and brown
brothers become targets.
Self defense exercised
with wide discretion.
Stop resisting, he said.
Stop resisting, he yelled
as he broke my nose.

I, a child, pinned
beneath three hundred pounds
of state sanctioned violence.
Children die with their hands up.
Children die in fear.
Our guardians seek the abyss,
look into the abyss,
find no monsters.
Yet, they fire.

Was it the crowd,
my color,
or the holiday season,
that stayed his gun?
Stop resisting he said.
But I will never stop.

Joshua Hegarty

ELEGY

I come here not to praise Law but to bury.
There is no honor in its failure or its death.
Law discarded burdens it was built to carry
until discarding of the burden of its breath.

There is no honor in its failure or its death.
There is no comfort for the victims, so neglected.
Until discarding of the burden of its breath,
there is no comfort for the wounded and dejected.

There is no comfort for the victims, so neglected
in a system built solely to protect.
There is no comfort for the wounded and dejected
in a system that refuses to respect.

In a system built solely to protect,
Law discarded burdens it was built to carry.
In a system that refuses to respect,
I come here not to praise Law but to bury.

Joshua Hegarty lives in St. Paul, Minnesota, where he currently attends Mitchell Hamline School of Law, while also being an MFA student at Hamline University. By the end of 2016, he hopes to be a bar admitted attorney working in employment and labor law. The RISE Anthology by VAGABOND, is the first publication of his work.

No Consequences

When there are no
consequences
monsters begin to recreate
themselves
grooming
malicious intent
with courtroom handshakes
made by misnomers
called justices of the
peace

When there are no
consequences
madmen patrol the streets
in search of blood
in search of victims
whose slaughter

means one less
two less
of the undesirable humanity
deemed unworthy
of a day in court
or
possibly a tomorrow

When there are no
Consequences
a mother's wail becomes
common
and a father's groan

the music of the
environmental landscape

When there are no
consequences
shadows are no longer

necessary
for broad daylight
becomes witness
to the shamelessness
of above the law antics

When there are no
consequences
talk of rights and
ambitions
fall upon deaf ears
whose cloning has
erased sentiment
but mass produced
twitching trigger fingers

When there are no
consequences
murderers donning the

wardrobe of the state
look mercilessly into the
camera
and say "yes"
and I shall again

Jeffery Martin

When there are no
consequences
a routine stop
no longer exists
it is now russian roulette
with one's fate
depending solely on
a self-proclaimed demi-god
with holster
and badge

When there are no
consequences

for you
it becomes a consequence
for me
when there are no
consequences
for you
it becomes a consequence
for me
when there are no
consequences
for you

it becomes a consequence
for me

When there are no
consequences
the necessary illusions
play out in
choreographed scripts

mouthed by the same
bad actors
and carried out
by the same bad
people
upon the lives
of a humanity
who want only
to be upholders
of the law
and not mere victims
of it

When there are no
consequences
law is infertile
and justice its
unborn child

Jeffery Martin: Poet, storyteller, author of eight books (4 books of poetry, 3 children's books and a play), uses life experiences as his inspiration behind what he shares with the world. His first book "Weapon of Choice" won the 2008 New Jersey Beach Book Festival for Best Book of Poetry and was also an Honorable Mention in New York and London Book Festivals of the same year. His book of poetry "As Sons Love Their Mothers" received Honorable Mention in the 2011 San Francisco Book Festival. He also received Honorable Mention for his children's book, "Silly Billy" in the 2011 San Francisco Book Festival.

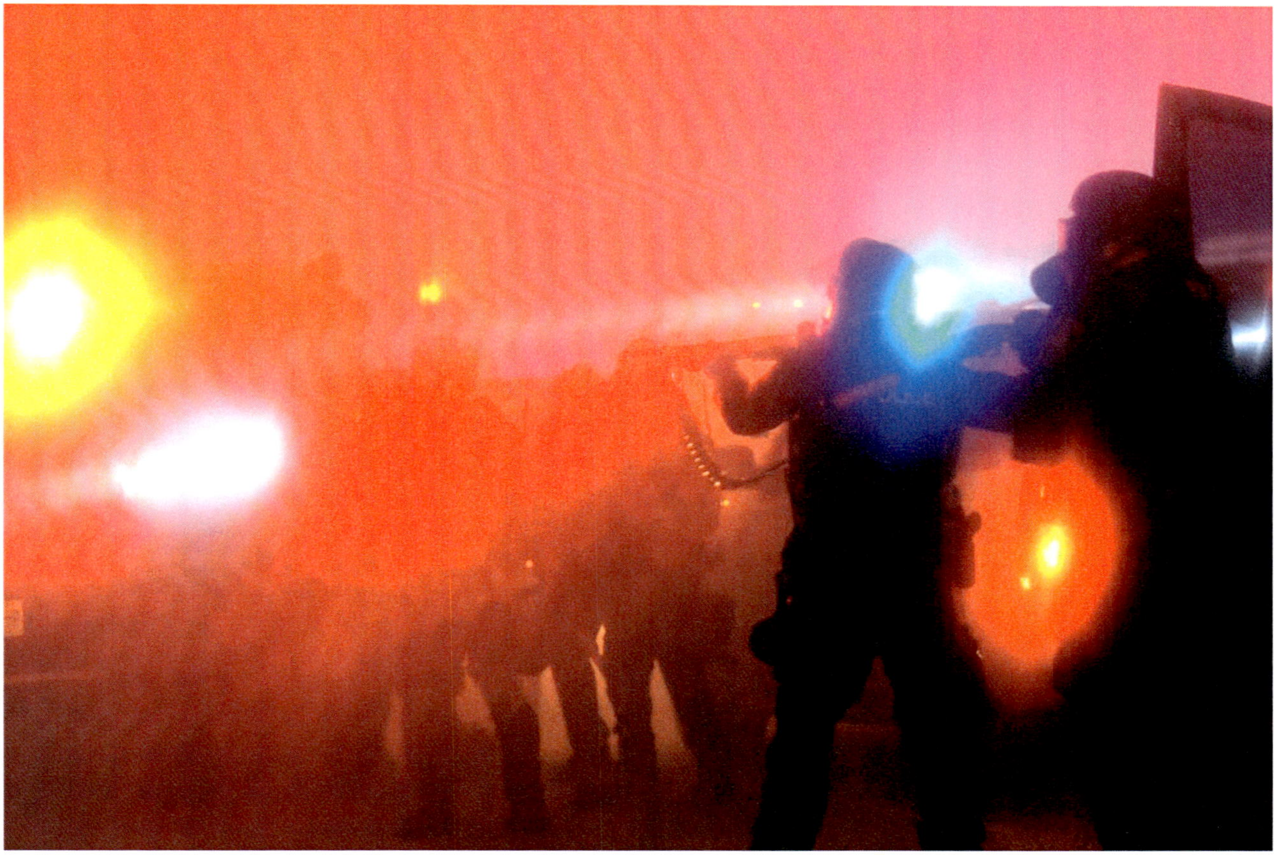

EPITAPH: IN THIS HISTORY

The grounds of Los Angeles are seeded with the dead
sprung falsely out of life at the hands of suicide;
trigger-happy thieves of perpetual night.
Oh how the darkness shades the alleyways:
old Chinatown laid waste beside Olvera,
brown kin, raided from hills
mowed in Dodger Blue.
Wasting curbs show lamps flickering to the follies of youth,
chasing family down with a gun. Soda caps
from ritualistic propaganda: "we from other sides, so we can't get along...,"
and it's not just in youth does death veil in disguise;
mass graves humming *no peace* host thousands of faces
making their voyage to the city of Angels.
Always broken knuckled and bloody; LA has lost her grip.
Union Station is the tombstone for hundreds of true *Angelenos;*
haloed *Indios*, swallowing sacred ground –
now trodden with rickety tracks and giant footsteps
of mass consumption.
The demon twin stands with grey skies,
malice to the mourning horns of *la mesa:*
los campecinos originales, saludos a tus hijas,
manos scattered without a wake.
The bones lay restless;
their names forgotten from their bodies.

Jessica M. Wilson Cárdenas

This is no genre of horror; this is a declaration of terror
that one day you may lay in your favored heaven,
only to feel the imprints of the bitter hell,
that claims your bones as its own.
Union Station – welcome to Los Angeles,
criminal penalties ignored with such *charming* scenery.

Jessica M. Wilson Cárdenas is the Founder and President of the Los Angeles Poet Society. She is a Beat Poet, with her MFA from Otis College of Art and Design, where she studied with Paul Vangelisti, and her BA from UC Riverside, where she studied under the wing of a Muse named Maurya Simon. She is honored to be a Poet Teacher and Area Coordinator for California Poets in the Schools. She is an activist and surrealist artist. Jessica is part of the world movement, 100 Thousand Poets for Change, organizing community events in LA; she also is part of the Revolutionary Poets Brigade in LA and dedicates her words to the freedom of Mohammad ibn Al Ajami, Ashraf Fayadh, and other humans being repressed and denied the right to speak their truth. Her new book of poetry, *Serious Longing*, is published by Swan World Press, in Paris, France, and is available now, which happily makes her an International Poet! www.lapoetsociety.org   www.jessicamwilson.com

Not Afraid to Speak the Truth

Let us not be afraid to speak the truth. America is not a free country. It is a country that pretends to be free. Do you have freedom of speech? Do you have freedom from religion? Do you have freedom from a government that will throw you in jail if you choose to not pay your taxes, unless you're a corporation, of course? The answer is a resounding no. You cannot have millions of unemployed, bankrupt, foreclosed-on, homeless, and poverty-stricken people and still have the audacity to say that you are free. You cannot have a central, private, banking system that is based on profit, loss, and perpetual debt and still proclaim to be free. You cannot have an obsessive surveillance spy-state monitoring your every movement and still think that you are free. You cannot have an oppressive criminal police-state that will arrest you, imprison you, or even kill you if you do not obey, and still feel that you are free. And you cannot have a monstrous, murderous, military machine based on endless war in the name of false power and false democratic domination, and dare to declare that you are still free. No, all these reflections from the cracked, shattered, one-way mirror called America are nothing but reflections of hypocrisy. And until we can see that, and indeed even say that, we will never be free. So let us not be afraid to speak the truth. For if we do not, all we have left are the lies and illusions that will destroy us.

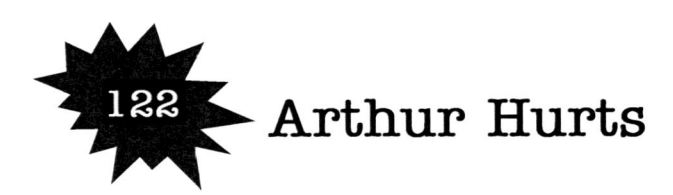

Arthur Hurts

THE BLOOD-SPLATTERED BANNER

oh say can you see
by the truth's fading light
what so loudly we hailed
at freedom's last meaning?
whose red stripes and blue scars
through the perilous fight
o'er the barbed wire we watched
as our tears were streaming
and the rockets' dead glare
the bombs bursting everywhere
gave proof with a fright
that the empire did not care
oh say does that blood-splattered
banner yet wave
o'er the land that was free
but is now so enslaved?

Arthur Hurts is a published author, decomposer, and free-thinking poelosopher. Also a political activist and social reformist, he is a veteran of the Occupy Wall St./Los Angeles movement and recipient of the prestigious Outcast of the Year award for the last twenty years in a row. A member of ASCAP since 1994, he is also the founding father of the Literary Outcasts of the World (LOW), and the Literary Society of Daredevils (LSD). In addition, he has recently been nominated for the No-Bull prize for exposing the hypocrisy and insanity of the human rat-race. Also known as Chief Stands Up to Bullshit, he is currently working on a bill to repeal the Federal Reserve Act of 1913, end the Infernal Robbery Service, eliminate the National Spying Agency, and establish the 666th amendment to legalize freedom. Yeah, he's about as free as you can get, without being dead, but he's also working on that.

Arthur Hurts

MOCKIT   *for Jack Hirschman*

                                      this little corporation went to market;
                                      this little corporation spied at home…
          these predatory corporations indulge in corporate cannibalism;
           Chinese corporations spy on us, slantwise, with perilous eyes…

this first president crossed the Rubicon;
this present president double-crossed the *publicum*…
this BIG government makes obscene practices legal;
these legal practitioners practice private contracting…

                                                         this little CEO
             made a millionaminute paying fourteencentsaday;
                          these U.S. corporations save in Bermuda;
                     these corporate yachts are sailing the Caimans;
          these multinational corporations paid no taxes to no-one;

big CEOs sit at the big Business Round Table;
these corporations share the Chamber of Commerce pot…
this CEO went to congress; this congress man went CIA;
[these corpulent exec's went obese]…

          these millionaire brothers bought a 'mans' with four bathrooms;
         these billionaire Brothers bought a congress with two chambers;
            these Warhol collectors bid millions for a bottle of '*Coke*'…
                 these Hedge Fund managers built PrisonsforProfit…

these Banking Brothers were too big to fail;
and, brother! – much too rich to jail!…
these Banksters had *us* bankroll their *Wall Street*;
[this little AIPAC dominates congress – andthensome]…

Ernest Rosenthal

> these enemy families were wiped out by drones;
> these Gitmo prisoners were *cleared*; – not *released*;
> these detainees are force-fed by torture;
> [billions of children are not fed at all]...

– then all corporations turned into persons:
no corpo-person suffered a stroke
no corpo-person developed a cancer;
no corporation died in the streets...

> all corporations did well, back in the market;
> no CEO went to jail...

[ADDENDUM]
...this little skittle-eating hoodie died,
looking suspicious to this big vigilante –
standing-his-ground – for life, liberty –
and the pursuit of hapless young blackness...

Ernest Rosenthal: Holocaust escapee and professor, does not consider himself a poet, but a polemicist, using poetic devices. Regardless, his words speak with such first-hand wisdom that it is difficult to accept them as anything other than truth. His major opus, *Not for Drones,* was published by VAGABOND in 2013.

WALL MART

strip frack machu picchu melon balls
ming hung macaroon
pitch black label
prime beef
christian mingled yeast snacks
blister sleeve private parts
russian dressing
korean darts
wheeled chairs hover
gadgets gum pumps
flat screen floss flowers
plaid shirt pants and
all beverage flapped left of
contacts pedicures pretzels
and pills:

    everything available
    by treaty
    by war
    by law
    by sneak
    by pressure
    on demand

    3 cents, 4 cents,
    occasionally a dime cheaper
    and the rare dollar loss-leader,
    all gathered in one tent
    precision pitched before
    you hit your town.

Peter Coco

quizno's goblets
ranchero-thighed
roam parking lot in
hip-hobble, cellulosed,
high jinx trek
to mobile cart clutching
of clockworked
cramps, scars, hives
and rashes stacked like deck –
shrink wrap shining –
picked, packed and sent
by distant forgotten
haunting each easy grip

blue vested weight lungs
droop the floor
cranked with survival
as doors sting open
non-stop…

                at those prices,
                who can resist?

Peter Coco: Lifelong Poet out of Newark, N.J., now writing and residing in Woodstock, New York. Peter participated in the Anti-War Movement of the mid to late 1960's; worked with ACLU to strike down unconstitutional 'Loitering' law in East Orange, New Jersey; was Editor-in-Chief of "Shapes of Things" Literary Magazine (1968-1970), Newark. In 1970, he worked with Amiri Baraka to save 135 acres of residential downtown Newark from Federal acquisition. Recently he has completed 3 volumes of short stories and Poetry collections chronicling the 1950's through present day.

A Short Poem

We are so rich what do we not deserve
We are so poor what should we not destroy

Mining Meaning

What does opal mean
In the madness of the brain
What does gold mean
In the madness of the heart
And what of diamonds
Cutting the glass of a dream

Patrick A. Harford is an Australian and earth scientist. His work takes him throughout the globe – so Patrick experiences many places and many forms of labor. Patrick has kept his youthful commitment to poetry for over 50 years now – through poetry Patrick chronicles those places of our world, its beauties, truths, and its iniquities. Patrick's poems present places and people. Most have scars from centuries of war and conflict, and the lashings of huge wealth amid grinding poverty. Patrick's poems are his guides, his models, and they deal with his demons.

Patrick A. Harford

COMPANY STORE

I've painted them a sign
It reads,
"Human souls for sale!"
I've sold my soul to the Company Store
Companies make billions off of me
Shopping
Consumerism
Corporatism
Advertising
I live in a Company Town
Wal-Mart
Target
Exxon-Mobil
Costco
And McDonald's
I live in a Company Town
It's where I eat, crap, and sleep
I work all day
And I work a hard day's night
Just to keep the bill collectors
At an arm's length
The bill collectors chase me down
Like zombies
And the cleverest ones on TV tell me
That they'll protect me
If I pay them for their protection
They call it,
"Re-financing and debt consolidation"
It's a protection racket
And I'm not gonna have it

Bills. Bills. Bills.
Loans and savings
Savings and loans
Good credit
Bad credit
Credit checks
Credit scores
Do you know the score?
A man outside of work
Told me
The Company
Wants to keep me in debt
Wants to make me feel trapped
Wants to keep me working
For the Company
'Till I collapse!
But maybe I'm really better off
In the hands of the Company
Times are tough
And they're looking out for me
Healthcare plan and 401k
Maybe I should be thankful
I'm not a coal miner
Or a sweatshop worker
I'm not hauling sixteen tons
Through darkness and soot
I don't live in a Nike Village
Making clothes and shoes
I'm free
I've got choices!
I've got options!

David A. Romero

I can go wherever I want
I can always leave
I just happen to really like this job
Actually, I hate this job
But I need this job
And besides, I'm saving up
For a big screen plasma TV
Plus, I'm trying to keep
The IRS off of my chest
And the Law off of my back
I can do whatever I please
In these sexy shackles of debt
Well, at least I can laugh at it!
Separation of State and Company
Honest business and America
Sometimes, I find myself wondering
If they might actually be in bed together
Exploiting my labor
Making a killing off of me
And all of my hard work
If there were to come a day of reckoning
When I could no longer pay them off
And the IRS
And the Law
Came to collect
Came to call
Came to take me away
They'd probably haul me off
To a private prison
Built and owned by the Company!
And I'd still be working for them!

Doing time
For their money!
I'm trapped, friend
There's no use in running
A man outside of work
Was yelling this out,
"The Company
Wants to keep you in debt!
Wants to make you feel trapped!
Wants to keep you working
For the Company
'Till you collapse!"
But, you know what?
I've got NO TIME to think
About all of that
I've got NO TIME to listen
To people like that!
I've got NO TIME to mess around!
Get all riled up
I've got to keep working!
To make my quota
To save up
To buy the things I can't afford...
A man outside of work
Was yelling out,
"You are not alone!
We are here!
We demand a better world!"
Maybe tomorrow
I'll start talking about tomorrow
Give me a break
I'm on break

I make little over minimum wage
I've got to work for today
I once cared
Once had a soul
But it's far easier
To stay comfortable
Be cynical
I have my pride
Jerk-offs of the world unite!
I no longer have a soul to save
It's every man for himself
So, don't you call on me for your movement
Or your Revolution
Because I won't go
Can't you see the billboards?
Don't you know that I live in a Company Town?
I sold my soul a long time ago
To the Company Store.

David A. Romero is a Mexican-American spoken word artist from Diamond Bar, CA. Romero has performed and led workshops at over 50 colleges and universities in over 15 states in the USA. Romero is the second poet to be featured on All Def Digital, a YouTube channel from Russell Simmons. Romero has opened for Latin Grammy winning bands Ozomatli and La Santa Cecilia. Romero has won the Uptown Slam at the historic Green Mill in Chicago; the birthplace of slam poetry. Romero has appeared in-studio numerous times on multiple programs on KPFK 90.7 FM Los Angeles. Romero's poetry deals with family, identity, social justice issues, and Latin@ culture. www.davidaromero.com

MY LANDLORD OTTO
(OR, THE 102 MAIN AVENUE BLUES)

My landlord Otto sez to me:
"Why ain't you happy as can be?
Just because I provide no heat
Ain't no reason to stamp yer feet.
Why, heat only ruins your bones,
Makes 'em dry and stiff as stones.
Ice-cold apartments make you strong,
Make yer body last so long.

"Who cares if yer in misery
So long as I can save money?
And don't you run to the Board of Health
Cuz I own them with all my wealth.
Ya see, that's how I get so rich:
by being an exploiting son-of-a-bitch!
Ya see, there's nothing you can do,
So just sit back and sneeze, Achoo!"

R. Bremner, of Glen Ridge via Lyndhurst, NJ, is a former cab driver, truck unloader, security guard, computer programmer, and vice-president at Citibank who writes of dead kings and many things he can't define, the clutter in your mind, and the color of time. He was in the first issue of *Passaic Review*, along with Allen Ginsberg. He has appeared in the *International Poetry Review, Oleander Review, Paterson Literary Review, Yellow Chair Review,* and *Poets Online* (18 times) and sundry elsewheres. Six of his verses were featured at the month-long Montclair Library Ekphrasis exhibit. He is a member of the Montclair Write Group and reads with the Red Wheelbarrow Poets. You're welcome to visit him at his page at Poets & Writers: www.pw.org/content/r_bremner

R. Bremner

Karma

Old and bent white men and women
hang on to the arms of their caregivers,
the same arms we take arms against
at the polls, the same arms we send
the police to grab, drag to a cell, or
shove over the border, the very same
pleading arms we turn our backs on now,
and shall miss when we are old and bent.

Gloria Vando's poems and books have won numerous awards and her work is widely anthologized, most notably on the Grammy-nominated *Poetry on Record: 98 Poets Read Their Work 1888-2006*. Her recent book, *Woven Voices* (Scapegoat Press), is a compilation of poems by three generations of Puertorriqueñas: her mother, Anita Vélez-Mitchell, herself, and her daughter Anika Paris. Gloria is publisher/editor of Helicon Nine Editions, contributing editor to *North American Review*, and cofounder of The Writers Place, a literary center in Kansas City. She serves on the board of the Venice Arts Council in L.A.

"EVERY MORNING I WAKE UP ON THE WRONG SIDE OF CAPITALISM."

What is It Like to be Black?

My white roommate
asked me what it was like to be black.

I quickly stopped coloring
brown in Ariel, the Disney-ed mermaid's, lines
I was in the middle of creating a cartoon
I could relate to
and get interrupted with this question,
too deep,
too invasive,
too confusing for me,
a girl from South Central
who never interacted
personally,
with white people until college,
to answer.
This question upset me
I didn't think I'd ever have to explain my culture to someone
completely oblivious
this question saddened me
she knew very little about black people

She asked me what it was like to be black,
in which I answered:

Black is the color of pressure
A pressing, withstanding
The color of survival and comebacks
Suffer
We are blamed – too quickly

Camari Carter

Killed – mercilessly
Underpaid
Untrusted
Muted
swept under welcome mats
America's step children
misunderstood
orphans
invisible
dismissed
yet, We are the creators
Unstoppable
Originators
Envied
copied from
Rich
Brimming with laughter
resourceful
colorful
culture
Innovative
Avant-Garde
Royalty

My answer to a question I thought
I'd never have to answer
an answer that satisfied and disturbed
an answer the left her regretful of asking
yet, she had a genuine longing to understand

I never apologized for my abruptness because I felt my description true
I am only left with the guilt of impatience
in an opportunity to peacefully explain
how the lack of my cultural representation in mainstream media
leaves white people to ask unreasonable questions.
I don't have to ask anything about her
her culture is overly saturated on television,
in malls,
grocery stores,
and freeway marketing.
Her question represented
the mass ignorance of black culture,
and that is what upset me.

However, at 17 years old,
I didn't have the capacity to say all of this.

THE NEW BLACK

is ripped jeans,
bold pink lips on plum skin
natural hair, twists, braids, bantu knots
bantu knot outs, braid outs, twist outs
shea butter, and evoo
the new thought ... new thought ... new thought
breaking free from great-great-grandma's
enslaved mind
releasing ourselves from granddaddy's
segregated patterns
We now mix patterns
red jeans, polka dot top, denim jacket
bold colored head wraps, maxi length skirts
sport blazer, black denim, wing tip oxfords

The new black
is community
a quilted unity
open mics at cafes
reciting poems
sippin' shiraz, cabernet sauvignon
discussing progression ... progression
learned lessons
forward moving sessions
by fire places
talkin' about how we matter
we now own homes ... homes
build homes
sell homes

Camari Carter

obtaining degrees, we are the new brilliant
Africana Studies to learn ourselves
teach ourselves
grassroots taking over, for ourselves

The new black
answers to our ancestors prayers
we embrace ourselves
taking risks
because we want to ... want to
chasing dreams
because we have to ... have to
no longer walking in fear

The New Black ... new black ... new black
don't stand down
don't back down
The New Black – strategic
innovative
investors
small business owners
large business owners
scholars
visionaries
social media gurus
poets
photographers
cartoonists
chefs
rulers

we live in etched concrete
we are books
look up!
we stand over you
we are rewriting history to what we want it to say
we are catalysts to a post-racial America
we are elites, regal beings
the standard of beauty
laughter in face of tragedy
always reemerging
   resurfacing
      resurrecting
you can't kill us
we are eternal

Camari Carter is a poet, photographer, natural hair stylist, and overall creative personality. Carter received her Bachelor's in Political Science and Masters in Organizational Management. She is an alum of the Community Literature Initiative and a house poet in Deitrick Haddon's League of Xtraordinary Worshippers. Carter's debut poetry book, *Death by Comb*, will release on May 18, 2016 at The World Stage Press. Visit www.camaricarter.com for more information.

Song from the Blood of Those Murdered

Why?
Why?
Why?
Why?
Come on
Come on, my brother
Come on, Black souls
Come on, mermaids

Gimme your Black eyes
Gimme your Black hair
Gimme your Black hand
Gimme your Black heart

Go to the enemy's land
    with all your gutsiness
Come on, Death

They're asking:
Where's your soul?
---I dunno. It's under the earth
    with the mermaids sounding.

They ask:
Where are your eyes?
---I dunno. On the mountain
    with the old men who are laughing.

They ask:
Where's your heart?
---I dunno. It's in the sea
    with the black spiders.

Why?
Why?
Why?
Why?

Go to the land of your enemy
    with all your gutsiness
Come on, Death

Diamanda Galás

Now I see the truth
---Death's gonna take you
And I see you two months buried
---Death's gonna find you
And I see its phalanx
---Why are you trying to escape?
And I see Death's hands
---Death's gonna have you
And I see my mother
---Death's gonna find you
Amen			Amen
Amen			Amen
Amen			Amen
Amen			Amen

Because don't you know we're returning
				one day?
Be careful: Because we don't forget!

Diamanda Galás is hailed as one of the most important singers of our time. Galás has earned international acclaim for her highly original and politically charged performance works. Notable among these are *Plague Mass*, *Defixiones: Orders from the Dead*, *Vena Cava*, *Schrei X* and *The Refugee*. Most recently, her performance work has concerned the musical setting of texts written by exiled poets and writers worldwide. She was the first recipient of the Demetrio Stratos award, Italy's prize for musical innovation. In 2010 Galás collaborated with filmmaker Davide Pepe to create the experimental sound and film work *Schrei 27*, an unrelenting portrait of a body suffering torture in isolation. In 2012 Galás began her collaborations with orchestrator Jon Ølvind Ness, resulting in a groundbreaking concert with the Norwegian Radio Orchestra at the Kanonhallen. Also in 2012 Galás presented a lecture-performance, *In the Mouth of the Crocodile*, at the "Weaving Politics" Symposium in Stockholm (alongside Julia Kristeva and choreographer William Forsyth), and opened Antony Hegarty's Meltdown Festival at the Southbank Centre in London.

Translated from Greek by Jack Hirschman, with Dimitri Charalambous

Orange Ain't the New Black

Orange ain't the new black, motherfucker
those aren't your new friends or even theirs.
There's no culture in these locked rooms.
There's nothing to enjoy or admire here,
this bullshit glorification of prison nation,
just another corporate toxin creep-sneaking
into the community corpus,
a social psychic infection.
– Seems us U.S. got the disease
that's fatal to freedom,
breaking up families
and harming children,
kids who can't see their daddies
who miss their moms.
The thing is, this is not a bug but a feature,
a self-perpetuating incarceration machine
with gears so finely adjusted you might not notice
they're just feeding on our fears,
pandering to our paranoia,
making sure bread winners can't get jobs
… or ahead … or even even.

In this real world jail food ain't catered,
it ain't even real food, it's just more white bread
and baloney served cold by the monster-mobsters of ARA
grifting government dollars for unbreakable trays
the sort of crap that oughta cost 50 cents
but it's your tax dollars so 50 bucks we pay
while kids go without books to school
and classrooms remain unheated,

Fred Dodsworth

the jail cells and pods are steamy-toasty
so your bright orange tee-shirt matches
those screaming orange socks inside
your orange plastic shoes
your permanent sealed plastic bracelet
also orange to match your Mr. Floppy, caution-colored pajama-pants
such as some Hollywood star might wear
while shopping in Paris or London or Rodeo Drive
if this were raw silk hand-sewn by Christopher Raeburn
rather just crappy cotton sewn by some sweatshop serf.

Watching pretty actors emote for the little big screen
ain't nothing like watching tattooed jail boys size each other up
figuring who they could take,
knowing there's no one in here to trust.
I saw a tattooed hard guy break and cry
because his baby mama wouldn't answer the letters he wrote
He hadn't heard a peep in nearly nine months
and him struggling over each and every word like a poet might
if that poet could just barely read and write.
Remember those school children without any books?
It's a feature, not a bug. It's designed that way.
The only booked he got was the one thrown at him
keeping the system fed in court that day
Three to five, out in two?
A full five or more if he plays the fool?
But what he says is he's learned to live inside,
it's going back to the streets that keeps him up at night.
What keeps me up at night is knowing I'm afraid
one of these men is just looking for the means
to spend the rest of his days locked up tight
because there's no one or where to go.

No jobs for cons. No work. No money.
No wonder they wind up back inside.

We're all getting use to the heavy steel doors
that close with a thud you feel more than hear
locked up tight the stark, empty corridors
that echo when you walk
while a thousand cameras watch.
Despite Ms Dolezal, no one's passing,
it's designed that way.
It's too easy to get use to waiting for the man
to let you in or out you can't
see who's watching who on all those screens,
who's flipping those switches,
shutting down the system
or setting you free.
The watching man
made sure nothing happened,
makes sure that nothing happens,
making sure that nothing ever happens.
It's a feature, not a bug.
It was designed that way.

Orange is not the new black, motherfucker,
though this black is what the future starts to look like,
not the darkness of not knowing but the stark
realization that the man's got a plan and you in it,
a deep mumbling hint that you, too, are redundant,
more fool-fuel than fuel-user
in this full on orange future they have planned
for each and every one of us
to come color-coordinated.

– These are the colors chosen for your season
orange wants to be the color of this and every future season.
This is a season that could easily last forever.
But orange is not your favorite color.
You never looked good in it.
It hints and tints and stains and casts
its pall over all and everything
that gets locked up and away.
Far from the family who might save you,
from the so-called friends who betrayed you,
from the sons and daughters who are ashamed of you,
from the husbands and wives who say
they don't really know you.
No. Orange is not the new black.
It's the new goddamn nightmare
and you best the fuck wake up.

Fred Dodsworth, a long time activist and journalist, is finishing his Masters in Creative Writing from SFSU. A poet since childhood, he is thrilled his short stories and poems are finally finding the light of day and hopes to complete his first novel this coming year.

147

Calling Car 2016

Catapulted into the criminal justice system by way of the slavery experience
Catapulted into the criminal justice sound-bite system
by way of pressurized economic exclusion

Noncompliance stranded between the galaxies
of accepted brother and stigmatized other
Compliance confronting the reasonable man doctrine
superimposed atop unreasonable economic conditions

Agent provocateurs constantly rearranging the carbon
fiber footprint, or fingerprint files
Agent provocateurs customizing each city with police interrogation,
beauty pageants, and the extracted roots of industry

Wild West theatrics sewn up into each tactical vets vamoose
Wild West influence still stalking the mass-psyche caught
between nano-particles and neon lights

Acquisition-avoidance culture finds another alternate route
for self-redirection back into neuroplasticity bliss
Acquisition-avoidance culture calls another private island real estate agent
floating over the down trodden suburb above the customized pesticide sprays

David S. Pointer was the son of a piano playing bank robber who died when David was 3 years old. David later served in the United States Marine Corps military police. Today, David serves on the advisory panel at "Writing for Peace."

David S. Pointer

BLACK MAGIC

I. police must think all
   black boys are born with nine lives,
   some with black magic.

II. cigars cost bullets,
    sacrificial organs, your
    spare of hoodoo spunk.

III. august in st. lou-
     is hot enough to boil boys
     in their own potions.

IV. 'cording to him black
    boy turned black/beast/coon/critter
    rushing to go ghost.

V. no ivory wish-
   bone is strong enough for the
   mother of color

VI. maybe we're all dead,
    black and brown zombies feeding
    off crooked pig's lead.

El Williams III is a St. Louis native and former member of the Eugene B. Redmond Writers Club. He earned his Bachelor of Arts degree in English, with a minor in Black Studies and a multicultural certificate from the University of Missouri-Columbia. He has read his poetry at events such as Break Word with the World and 100 Thousand Poets for Change. He currently works as the Director of Graduate Support for Loyola Academy of St. Louis, a Jesuit middle school for boys, where the mission is to break the cycle of poverty through education.

HOMEGROWN

Years ago my stepfather,
a white man with a well-manicured backyard,
planted a garden with the same enthusiasm
of a school child on the first day of summer.

These days that garden births tomatoes by the handful
and enough grapes to make gallons of wine in the basement.
My stepfather likes his food homegrown,
enjoys the familiar taste that comes from knowing
it all came from his own soil.

My mother,
a white woman drinking a glass of her husband's wine,
is sitting on the couch
when a headline flashes across the TV screen.
Another shooting.
Twelve dead.
The suspect in custody
is described as a lone wolf,
a mentally ill, former football star.
When the photos are released,
he is being led away in a bullet proof vest,
as if his whiteness
had not saved him already.

She will not call this an act of terrorism,
this almost daily bloodshed.
This is just the way things are in America.
Another shooting.
Rinse, repeat, go back to work.

Dylan Garcia

Go back to sleep.
Ignore it all in the morning,
or until the next explosion of gunfire,
or until the next black man is shot while handcuffed,
or until the next country is bombed by the US
in the name of freedom.

September 11, 2001 was the first time
I ever heard the word "terrorism."
I was twelve years old
and before the dust from the Twin Towers had settled,
adults were scrambling to help me understand
this was just a tragedy,
this was not supposed to happen here.
These were terrorists, not Americans.
As if the two were mutually exclusive.

Terrorists, I was told,
had dark skin and wore turbans.
I grew up afraid of people who did not look like me
because America refuses to admit
we create monsters ourselves.

This country has a terrorism problem,
but it is homegrown, not imported from Syria or Iraq.
The skeletons in our closets look like
politician in suits with murderous intent,
trigger-happy police officers,
and white men toting guns
into schools and movie theaters.

When my stepfather starts thinking about planting green beans
he stands in the backyard surveying the options of the land.
He has no fear of what grows here.
He doesn't think about the white men in his neighborhood,
their guns or their hateful ideas.
He is too busy considering how the sky might swell
with brown men in hijacked planes
while his hands are covered in dirt.

Dylan Garcia is a performance poet and political organizer from Rockford, Illinois. He has had poems published in Radius, Words Dance, Wicked Banshee Press, and The Legendary. He is a member of Fight Imperialism, Stand Together (FIST) and hopes his poetry can help educate working class people.

Cycles of Murder in Fort Hood

"License, insurance, registration"
Grinning Jack O' Lantern hollow
Flickering with inner light of death
Blue pretender Sir Lancelot of over ripe rotting righteousness
Slow motion hand reaches to retrieve Babylon's bureaucratic paper chains
"It's almost 2 A.M."
I'm a wage slave condemned to the midnight shift, sir
"What! We're all free," as the hand slides down to the death dealer

Flashback crashback, sadsack

Momma rising before the roosters sang welcome to the rosy sun
Ironing, cleaning, attending children delegated to the shelf of neglect
Matron Mistress voyaging daily on the cruise ship U.S.S. Self Indulgence
Paying pittance because emptiness is a vacuum sucking sordid superiority
For your servitude, starvation wages and give me your best
You're a benevolent matron of Mother Teresa kindness grin
While I fend, pretend unable to contend
Taught undeniable equality
Contrasting the visual mansions of glory
To dilapidated rain leaky, wind creaky shacks
My history a dark mystery, a faint foot note in unreadable font
Sadistic psychopaths with super nova fiery wraths
Robber Barons as bullets articulate reality in crimson blood
Meanwhile dual autobiographies
One in pencil one in golden pen
Mammy, 'part of the family', tossed out like stinking garbage as child comes of age
I struggle, teachers ambushed by swarming children of common curiosity
Miss Proper's precious 'problem child'
Tutored in technical tune up to speed

John Kaniecki

So here I am at community college part time, giving forty hours plus
The wallet fills to empty into bills, constant flux
While my equal brat on daddy the donor's domineering dime
Worships Bacchus in his Greek society well prepared with old exams
Irregardless think thank philosophical fascist formulas
Puts dogs with minds infested by swarming hornets of hatred
On a vacant isolated street somewhere in anonymous suburbia
Flashing red lights beacons of something wicked this way comes
Pistol armed lethal termination at an itchy twitchy finger
In calm nervous panic a man condemned at first sight
Volumes of hypocritical prejudices written in victim's life blood
Hoping, coping, saying ignorant silent prayers to anything greater lending an ear
Bang, bang, bang a trinity of total tragedy

Early report, breaking news, dynamiting a newlywed's dreams
Like a crystal chandelier shattering
She'll walk barefoot, tiptoeing through torment perpetually
"A routine traffic stop turns deadly!"
Blares the boob propaganda tube
Bloggers spin with forked tongue sin
Suspended duty with pay,
A vacation to a sunny spot to slip the heat
Anger, outcry, another name in a litany of instant lynches
T i m   e, a deterrent tactic,
Investigation by blood brothers in the identical thin line of blue
One living testimony tips the already slanted scales of justice?
Insufficient evidence, no charges

Enter now lustful lawyers, bottom sucking up for some scum
As if money could provide tender caresses and faithful whisperings of
"I love you"
She kneels at the grave stone, worshipping the god of agony in mainline purity

In the greatest of misfortunes the Mobius Strip never ends
Somewhere in the interior of Fort Hood
Next tragic night, next tragic time
"License, insurance, registration"

If the workers take a notion,
They can stop all speeding trains,
Every ship upon the ocean
They can tie with mighty chains.
Every wheel in the creation,
Every mine and every mill,
Fleets and armies of the nation,
Will at their command stand still.
— Joe Hill

The Worker Shall Rise

Help wanted ads they no longer exist
It'll get better politicians insist
Take a look at history for our guide
If we stick together we can't be denied

You say heaven is beyond the skies
Take a back seat I can hear your lies
The worker shall rise, the worker shall rise
In the heat of the street hear our cries
The worker shall rise, the worker shall rise

Living in the parks wandering the street
Longing for some warmth or a morsel to eat
They took it serous when banks went broke
Now that it's the people they laugh like a joke

You say heaven is beyond the skies
Take a back seat I can hear your lies
The worker shall rise, the worker shall rise
In the heat of the street hear our cries
The worker shall rise, the worker shall rise

Share the wealth our slogan ringing so true
Power to the people that means me and you
Capitalism the religion of greed
Socialism giving as there is a need

John Kaniecki

You say heaven is beyond the skies
Take a back seat I can hear your lies
The worker shall rise, the worker shall rise
In the heat of the street hear our cries
The worker shall rise, the worker shall rise

Big business bribes everyone taking lead
The government is sick everyone got greed
The common man has a plan of solution
Brothers and sisters time for revolution

You say heaven is beyond the skies
Take a back seat I can hear your lies
The worker shall rise, the worker shall rise
In the heat of the street hear our cries
The worker shall rise, the worker shall rise

John Kaniecki is an author and poet. He has two poetry books "Murmurings of a Mad Man" and "Poet to the Poor, Poems of Hope to the Bottom One Percent." In addition he has a science fiction collection entitled Words of the Future. John's poem *Tea with Joe Hill* won the Joe Hill Labor Poetry Prize. John's work has been published in over seventy outlets. John resides with his lovely wife Sylvia in Montclair, New Jersey. He volunteers as a missionary in the inner city of Newark and hopes one day his writing will have a positive impact on the world.

Ode to a Tomato Truck

It must be told what happens in late summer.
They roll like unholy thunder through
the highways of The Valley, dropping
their red bombs along the berm.
The bumps throw a bunch more across
the gravel to become a pox upon the road.
The asphalt is sick from the harvester's
excess. Each conveyance carries its
transfusion of cells. Each red globe
is the flesh of the sun's dream,
and it races to the cannery
on the back of the two-trailer beast.
Oh how the windshields shine!
How the giant tires spin like
the maniacal black eyes of wild animals,
and the rigs sing the song of the pavement saw,
digging into the hot-baked surface
of the empty lane ahead. It's this song
that keeps the drivers awake: one who
used to work the rail yards, another
who wants shorter waits between loads,
one more who worries about cargo theft.

They all fear the tale of the tip over
and some wiseacre making a crack about
salsa with bits of road-kill. They are haulers
in the high seat on the newly extended
Camino Real. They tow those Romas
to be skinned, diced and puréed for soup.
Mmm-Mmm good. God bless
the Campbell's plant for its
smooth red stew that doubles in a pinch
as blood on an old white work shirt.

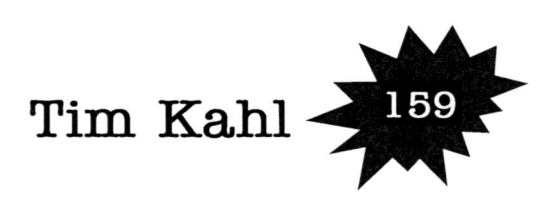

Tim Kahl

After the Wheatland Hop Riot

The raisin crop in Turlock was in dire need of hands.
A boy's power in the fields measured itself in dollars.
Old Glory floated in the breeze and the school authorities
sent them on to gladden the hearts of pea growers.
Deaf mutes from Berkeley came to harvest Yolo County.
The Woman's Land Army of America, California Division
was formed for the duration of the war. Their duty
fortified the slogan: if you can't fight, farm.
There were flickers of strikes that were followed by
arrests. Detectives served as deputies to bring
the agitators to trial. The deputies also stood along
the bridge to the capitol with their rubber bludgeons
and kept the blanket stiffs and bohunks from
crossing the river. They stayed vigilant, and with their
pick handles invented their own brand of vigilantism.
Transients were starving in the great valley of
the San Joaquin, transients in the season of heavy rains
and floods who might be swallowed up by
fertile earth to someday sprout up into
their full discontent, old city oaks amid
the slickened streets. They train the traffic
to see the worn down groove on the way to gain.

Tim Kahl [www.timkahl.com] is the author of *Possessing Yourself* (CW Books, 2009), *The Century of Travel* (CW Books, 2012) and *The String of Islands* (Dink, 2015). His work has been published in *Prairie Schooner, Drunken Boat, Mad Hatters' Review, Indiana Review, Metazen, Ninth Letter, Sein und Werden, Notre Dame Review, The Really System, Konundrum Engine Literary Magazine, The Journal, The Volta, Parthenon West Review, Caliban* and many other journals in the U.S.

Tim Kahl

An Untold Fire is Dead

He promised me, on his word of honor,
to let me work as human –
and work high as a mountain. And stack diamonds high as the sky.
I asked my boss: "why am I treated differently?"
He answered "work like each day was the last day."
I replied "Each day was the only day."
Something unavoidable is lost like the morning mist;
dying in a gust of endless void.
I need my life back.
He yelled, you just "looked wrong"; you possess no superior color!
A deep and descending warmth potentially, a presence
of internal tragedy crushes my hut; it stings with bleakness.
Perhaps it was burning; I was unaware of it.
More than a lot has departed; departed with the wind,
spread into the cloud. My vigor distorted with fear; stood apart
grown old beyond my years.
All the plagues of this distressed world
are carved on my arms.
labor recognizes my forlorn face as he
looked over my shoulder.
He shouted "pull yourself up, dignity is not here,
labor is unlike slavery."
My weary arms overburdened with useless submission
fell out of my tree.
I often confuse my arm with my tree branch;
I grab it and it becomes rustling branches.
My presence will linger
and mature and mature
to trouble the cold world,
with heart forever closed. An untold fire is dead.

Ayo Ayoola-Amale

THE DAWN OF MY BEING

Out of Africa we all sprung
because I am duskier so am asked to clean up the kitchen after each meal.
I scrubbed everything and everywhere and grew strong.
Without any understanding
I live in a shack; deep-rooted divisions.
My skin has a deep mind that touches everything.
Where is the grave for black skin?
Where is a life that never passes away?
Where is the one that came not out of the common dust?

Ayo Ayoola-Amale is the Lead Mediator/Arbitrator, First Conflict Resolution Services Inc. She is a law lecturer, Faculty of Law, Wisconsin International University, ADR Practitioner, Ombudsman and a Poet. Ayo is the Founder/President, Splendors of Dawn Poetry Foundation, Vice-President, Poets of the World. (Movimiento Poetas del Mundo) and Coordinator World Poetry Movement. Ayo has several local and International certificates in creative writing and has attended various Local, National and International Workshops and Seminars on creative writing and presentation. She has been a guest poet at International Poetry Festivals. A spoken-word and performance poet, Ayo has written volumes of poetry, a short story and a play. Her aim is to employ poetry for positive social change. Her poems and other literary works have appeared in several international and national anthologies, magazines and journals. She is a recipient of several awards. www.splendorsofdawn.org www.growintopeace.wordpress.com

Ayo Ayoola-Amale

Do They Know Who They Are?

Those out there despise my town.
They fear revenge
from their own antagonisms
inflicted back onto them.

Is their problem psychological?
political? cultural? or just
plain economics?

Let's not think too hard
about what hardly gets
thought about at all.

They hate pigment in the skin.
Hate when those
so genetically scarred
behave as they had expected.
Hate even more when
they aspire to respectability,
that trait they cling to
in the absence of any other.

But I have started to confuse my they-s.
Let me run to the mirror
so that I can tell them apart.

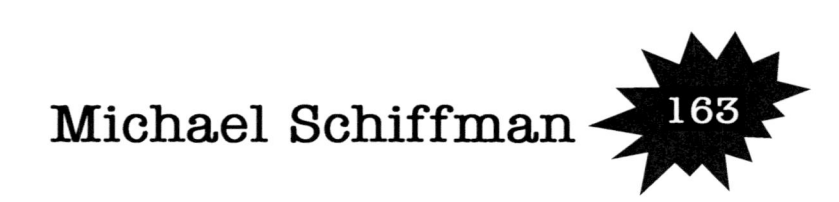

Michael Schiffman

The Sewing Floor

The women wait at their machines
and chat. Whatever thoughts they have
are left unspoken: the stale, yet fervent,
hope for a profitable day:

a few small bundles, fewer stripes,
plaids, changes of thread, a share
of sturdier fabrics, twills and woolens,
to ease the stress of sewing at high speed.

The wooden floors creak, as super-
vision and bundle boys stack work
in good order. The parts will meet
their partners down the line.

The bell sounds. The lunatic pace commences.
The slow, the fast, the quick, the nimble,
the blundering and the temperamental,
humanity as seen through the prism

of piece work. The clock and its second hand,
judge and arbiter. A routine, paradox-
ically onerous and beloved,
a tempestuous fraternity.

And the cacophony of language!
Italian, Spanish, Greek, Portuguese,
a bit of German against a backdrop
of English. City people from nearby

Michael Schiffman

ethnic enclaves, others from further away.
The business is shuttered now, as the city
goes on collapsing around it.
The railroad siding, once active next door

at the mattress factory, now rusts, its shame
buried among abundant weeds. The work,
the workers, have mostly disappeared.
Who would want to sew for a living?

or press? or cut? In a few years
the building will be razed. In its place
a parking lot for the community
college since founded on all this debris.

Michael Schiffman: I am a seventy-three year old poet. In the course of my life I have had three careers: in academia (a dissertation, unfinished, at Columbia on Mark Twain's Humor, where I also began writing poetry), in the men's tailored apparel industry, and as a wine salesman. Since retirement I have attended Bread Loaf three times and also the New York Summer Writers Institute where I've sat in Frank Bidart's workshop. I spend more and more time writing and reading, although I still peddle a little Pennsylvania wine to my old customers.

166

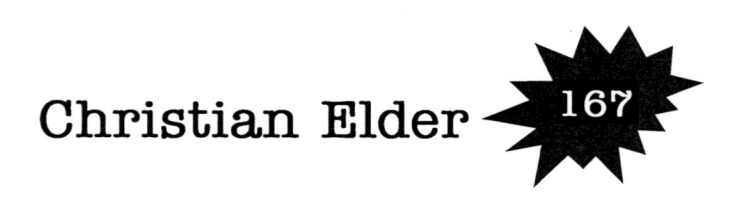

#ANINSIGNIFICANTMAN

i killed
an insignificant man
    with a burst of sleep
    and bird shit
    and subprime loans
i brought him
a plague
    of board room meetings
        and faxed him
    a wilderness of hurt
i nailed
his wife
to a rotted door
    with a ballpoint pen
        split her open
    and wiped her
        inalienable rights
        on an unborn fetus
i slow walked him
thru the supreme court
    and got my mojo working
    turned the roulette wheel on
        KKK
        street
and shifted
voting rights
    back
for decades
i held

a little brown boy
    down
    last summer
        and stole his sugar
    made him grit it out
        made him into a man
        behind   the schoolyard

warned him
    not to say a word
or i'd get his mommy
    and daddy
    deported
i flew a kite
like a wedge
    caught in a startled sky
    and a drone
    fucked it up again
    i cried like before
but this time
    i posted it all
    on Twitter

Christian Elder

i finally broke down
       and went to see the counselor
       on campus
       my body parts
       were oily
       and divided
       and the big game
       was tomorrow
we talked about my future
       and we figured we shouldn't make waves
i lived

       in the bunker
       of my white jesus
       rewriting the constitution
             under great duress
                   dripping from
LSD

and tripping balls
       while streams
             of mega data dreams
                   kept us snowed in
                         a backroom
                             owned by the NSA

we kept them there
    waiting for
    free
    dumb
        to ring
i protested
    with the sick
i came
    with the lame
i twitched
    and i occupied
    but i couldn't find coverage
i reported
    the news
    and the defenseless
        howled
    crazy into the white night
        until they were pounced on
            by the national guard
                and bludgeoned
            to a hard

    stop
i raised my hands
    in front of the keyboard
    and thought man
    please don't do it
i saw that nigga
and hashtagged him
        at least six times
    # # # # # #
    scroll down
    Michael
    Brown

you will turn

over
like another distraction
    in the discussion
    bleeding out
from our
    rights
        as one people
but until then
    you're trending this week
down the middle
    of the road

PEOPLE OF NO COLOR

it was the year
white people
didn't know

it was the moment
they wiped
america back to zero

it was the days
they slipped
in the polls

it was the path
to the white house
on the right wing

it was the minute
men claimed
militia lives matter

it was the hour
for white power
cut to camera two

it was body cameras
and dash cameras
and old west blowdowns

it was the week
to attack sikhs for muslims
and muslims for paris

it was the market
and weighing in on china
and speculate this

it was disconnection
and who made
all these silly devices

it was what
enter vain meant
and why you get all the shit

it was why reagan
was never termed
a petulant child

it was whitewater
for the clintons
and brown for flint

it was monsanto
and all these frigging gmos
and just fuck it

Christian Elder

it was an answer
for cancer
like they don't have it now

it was isis
and captain marvel and
why syria is our graphic novel

it was the time
good faith couldn't pass
a gall stone in congress

it was the year
that white people
didn't know

for the love of god

does anybody know
how the hell to tell them

Christian Elder is a playwright, painter, and filmmaker living in the San Fernando Valley. His poems have appeared in many publications, including *Saturday Afternoon Journal*, *Blue Satellite Magazine*, *Art/Life Magazine*, and *Coiled Serpent: Poets Arising from the Cultural Quakes & Shifts in Los Angeles*. His work has also been featured on LA radio's Poet's Cafe on KPFK and KXLU's Echo in the Sense.

172

The Street Vote Arcane

1.

They came in the night,
breaking the window.
They ate my child,
tore up my poems,
left me shivering, naked,
called me Scum
and left in a shout.

They're no seasons,
wear definite looks,
are quick with yesterday,
a wing of the church,
the spider shrine.
They're everywhere and no one
can see them. They bug out.

The poor eat the air
and live on high
in cellars of drunken mouths.
The strikers beaten
by police in Detroit,
the hair pulled along
the ground in California,

the moon that tastes bitter
in pussies of desire---
O, I got much mouth
to say here,

intricate ears
and a tradition
of genuine wires.

I got my doll
and my monkey,
the joint and
the illusion of it
at my torn elbow,
the slam that's slammed
and the slum under

Calamine on my chin
like a pimple of bop,
an atomic blister,
a deep wound
from an Apple
that sticks
in my throat.

2.

I'm neither an elephant
nor an ass. I love infant joy
and the happiness of socialist
dreaming. My eye sees
PARTISAN and my I says Yes.
But for that we go deeper,
we go under the ground

Jack Hirschman

of any splinter in the wood
of this tunnel.
We want death out
of the eyes of the child,
out of radical mind.
We want people
to unscrew their heads,

lift out the bomb,
to a man, to a woman.
We want people,
from top to bottom,
to doff their White House
for the first time,
take off its car,

steal the steel
from under
the sickeningly
deranged gaze
of the munitionary
powers. We want
the hearts of the People

to lift off into the space
left by their throwaway
duds, and leave behind
the whodunit fixations
and foolish accusations
against their very own
selves.

3.

Down here, in this booth
where we're voting,
we're also all over the sky,
the land, the cities.
We're down like an erection
of tenderness out of the stiff
cock-arm of rigid waste.

We're down so high
the roots of the earth
are climbing our arms
like snake-vines
nuzzling us like children
of cat magic
----animal kind---

returned to our cause,
after so much belly
and so much
exasperated wind,
in the form of
the Red air
we cast our vote for,

the re-dare every minute,
the *raduga* span
of the Song
throwing its arms around
any color of peace
because all of us at last
have found its true center.

THE MIWOK ARCANE

1.

The crime now is the lie
and its many states,
as many as compose
its myriad cities, suburbs,
towns and podunks.
And it's over over here.

We not only live with them
in the new geography of
money. We contribute
to them our chisels, hustles,
the stash-mouth economy
of the streets.

We're subdivided projects
never to be built, connected
to hooks yanked smack into
the middle of the packing
house of the spoiled rotten
porn meat of the sun.

2.

It's begun to dawn: how
treacherous, after all, the
whole wine-soaked, dope-
smoked nightmarish story
of the mangled psyches of
the lonely ones of drink,

of the long ago goodbye
I said to the you, with your
umlaut eyes and stunned
little lips of an Indian of
love in a hustler's progress,
of literal cold-ass turkey.

A stoned work for the new
New Deal and, at the other
end, moral camps for the
up-tighters. To abandon the
poor? Make like poverty
don't exist, they say.

The oil-sheen's in every
tree: book saps you'll be,
they say. The absolutely
most extraordinary country
on earth, they say persistently.
But on any indigenous day,

you'll see the truth by the way
the faces turn away from what,
in you, is unstoned, not up-tight
and poor as a consonant without
a vowel, or as if you said your
mother's an iguana in Merida.

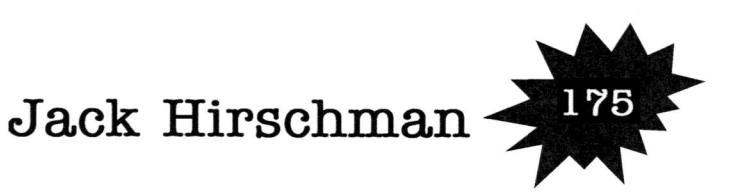

Jack Hirschman

3.

So, yes, this land is your home
and can't be taken from you
because they've locked it in
the peace of war and death;
each year more and more
is their money not yours,

and drone skulls pile up into
pyramids, towering columns
for the nothing their eyes are
forever interested in; pile up
as high as the lies exploding
into bummers of fireworks.

The church for the salvation
of cheap labor has broken
our dark mahogany backs,
shoved coins into the slits
of our women, made them
runaways and fugitives.

And we who were the Black
Indians of North California,
we, the Miwok, are still the
Miwok, and in our stampfoot
happiness, pounding chants
we kiss the skins of the drums

for Chocuyen, Timalakees,
Petaluma, Yolhios, Oleomi,
Tamalanos, Tumalehnias,
Baulines, Oleomipalies, and
here, friend fearing technology's
myriad screens have overrun

our visions and hopes, I give
you a black obsidian stone,
tell you the creek still runs by,
our door's still a chimney. Trees
are in slender bloom. The woods
still hold much deer. Welcome.

Jack Hirschman is an American poet and social activist who has written more than 50 volumes of poetry and essays. Born in New York City, Hirschman received a Bachelor of Arts from City College of New York in 1955, and an A.M. and Ph.D. from Indiana University in 1957 and 1961, respectively. When he was 19, he sent a story to Ernest Hemingway, who responded: "I can't help you, kid. You write better than I did when I was 19. But the hell of it is, you write like me. That is no sin. But you won't get anywhere with it." Hirschman left a copy of the letter with the Associated Press, and when Hemingway killed himself in 1961, the "Letter to a Young Writer" was distributed by the wire service and published all over the world. Jack is also co-founding member of the Revolutionary Poets Brigade and the World Poetry Movement.

Someone Said the Sun Had Died

Someone said the Sun had died	Hanno detto che è morto il sole
the Silence is dead	è morto il silenzio
ripped by vowel of wind	lacerato da vocali di vento
on the skin of the Sea	sulla pelle del mare
bare clothes and empty shoes	abiti nudi e scarpe vuote
are mountains of nothing	sono monti di niente
between spectra-house and bone-trees	tra spettri di case e alberi d'osso
God has been silent	Dio ha taciuto
whenever a lamb has whimpered.	ogni volta che un agnello ha vagito.

Maria Elena Danelli, Italian poet and theatrical set designer, graduated from *Brera*, and worked for many years at the *Scenografie Ercole Sormani* in Milan (it was the oldest laboratory stage design born in 1838), collaborating with Theaters around the World and movie sets. She has participated in many solo and group exhibitions. The publisher Alberto Casiraghy hosted some of her works on his *Pulcino Elefante* editions. Maria founded an editorial and artistic project with Gaetano Blaiotta, called *GaEle Edizioni*, in Valcuvia.

Maria Elena Danelli

LOLITA LEBRON (Puerto Rican Independence Fighter)

Back back back
to New York in the fifties
they were the times of hate
the times of fear.
Witch-hunters flying
from town to town
from Washington to the electric chair
where the Rosenbergs sat.
On their execution day
people stood in solidarity.
The minutes till their death
counted over the loudspeaker.
Ten
nine..............
the police
cutting the microphone.
By person to person relay
the word was passed
like a whisper heard by thousands
the chant of life's last moments.
"Eight" runs through the crowd
then "seven" /
the song of resistance.
Six / five /
"no names"
four / three / two /
shock
electric shock
and then they were dead.

Those were times of fear,
times of hate,
teachers signing loyalty oaths.
Fear
that they may not teach
what the system would preach.
Front page headlines
naming communists / banning books.
Witch-hunters flying in the moonlight.
The people were picking up the tab.
It was all on the expense account.
"Have plane fare, will testify."
The professional witness,
trained by Judas,
And will you name names?
And will you name names?
Names on blacklists
Attorney General's lists
subversive activities list
Didn't you belong to this committee?
Didn't you sign that petition?
Didn't you spend many years
in the company
of a suspected communist
who was your mother?
Smith Act trials and jailing.
"Are you now or have you ever been?"
And will you name names?
And will you name names?

Nina Serrano

The witch-hunters flew
to the world of make-believe
the movies, the pictures, the stars,
the Hollywood Ten.
"Not me, couldn't be."
Then who?
Point your finger at your ex-wife
your enemies
and you can keep on making
payments on your swimming pool,
and winning prizes.
And will you name names?
And will you name names?
Those who didn't went to jail.
Take the key and lock 'em up.
The witch-hunters flew
in the dark and repressive fifties.
The 20th century just about halfway through
when the Taft-Hartley Act tied knots
around the picket lines
binding union power
purging unions with
"Are you now or have you ever been?"
Do you think he is?
What did she say? and to whom and when?
Labor and management must become one happy family,
signing sweetheart contracts.
But it was hard to have a happy family
on such a lousy salary
where Lolita worked.

The machines whirred in the garment factory
the faster the better
the fewer stitches to the inch
the greater number of workers per square foot.
Pay them by the piece.
Clothes are going to make it big this year,
as we go from wartime shortage
to the new look of the consumer society.
Skirts were longer again.
Women left the wartime plants
for flowerpots in the kitchen.
"Homework, I want to do homework,
instead of an office I want
to work home."
Lolita worked in one of those factories
where bits of thread
floated through the air.
The benches by the sewing machines
filled by the latest immigrants,
Borinqueños, Puerto Riqueños,
migrating when there was no work,
no harvest.
When the colony was squeezed
so hard
it spit out its population.
Lovely island of coco palms and sea,
wet song of the rain forest.
"Pepsi Cola hits the spot"
mingles with tropical laments.
La lee lo lei lo lai
La lee lo lai

Lolita looked at the moon
on hot nights
from her tenement roof.
She saw the witch-hunters fly by
but paid them no mind.
Her mind was on cutting the chains
tying her green island
to the greedy mainland,
pouring concrete on her country's fertile land
building military bases and factories,
sucking its rum
and sugar cane.
She was set on freedom.
She would bet on freedom.
Take a chance
that the world would know her dream.
"Crazy-Loca" they called her.
When US bombers are blasting Puerto Ricans
and US citizens don't even know about it,
"What can one isolated act do?"
She made her plan with three others.
They needed a gun
to shoot off the word.
The word had to be heard –

Puerto Ricans wanted their independence.
"Are you sorry for what you did, Miss Lebron?"
"I am not sorry for anything I do
to free my people."
And you, Irvin Flores
and you, Andres Figeroa Cordero
and you, Rafael Cancel Miranda?"

"No, we are not sorry about what we do
to free Puerto Rico."
No need to name names
"I take responsibility for all,"
she said,
in her accented English.
Elvis Presley howled
"I'm nothing but a hound dog"
and the shake, rattle and roll
of the yeah, yeah, yeah
was creeping into the music
and the witch-hunters flew straight
into the fires of the thaw
of the cold war.
Juke boxes turned their colored lights on.
TV sets filled every tract home and tenement.
Cars filled every street and parking lot.
The air turned black.

Peace in Korea.
War in Viet Nam,
always war.
The witch-hunters were howled out of town
by crowds of demonstrators,
protestors.
The witch-hunters circled around
and landed safe
in their offices.
Lolita went on a hunger strike
to back up the prisoners' rebellion
at Attica.
Meanwhile freedom is a constant struggle
and the witch-hunters are just waiting,
waiting ...
waiting for you.

Nina Serrano is the author of the poetry trilogy "Heart Suite" consisting of "Heart Songs, Collected Poems of Nina Serrano, 1969-1980," Editorial Pocho-Che, 1980; "Heart's Journey, Selected Poems 1980-1999," Estuary Press; and "Heart Strong, Selected Poems 2000-2012." She is the winner of the 2013 Artist Embassy International Book Award for Heart's Journey and the Josephine Miles PEN Oakland Award 2014 for Heart Strong. She is the radio host/producer of the KPFA-fm, "La Raza Chronicles," a weekly Latino magazine program, and "Open Book/Poet to Poet," a monthly literary program.

Rosetta's Stone

Our greatest fear is that we never reach the highest of peaks
Fighting against the fading of our existence forgetting to live
It is the ing we forget to do
The action that follows the words in which define our time spent dying
A heart beats roughly two billion times if we're lucky
So I dance to the percussion of this ocean of blue running through me
We are miracles
Death is the greatest burden we bare yet I am more afraid of forgetting to unleash hurricanes back into the universe
Fearful of becoming so dormant that I forget that I am a descendant of giants
A continuation of a story seldom spoken
Our history is cozied under a blanket full of small pox
Stifled beneath broken treaties
Waiting to be heard by deaf ears
Reflection is a song best sung in the light
Atop the crimson stained battlefields where life once existed in harmony with mid-summer breezes inspired by the flutter of a butterflies wings
Illuminated by 50 stars
We are the reverberation of 1492
Redskins once existed
They were newborns littered amongst the plains like the pedals of daisies torn from their roots
Discarded in the name of destiny
Their story rests in the clouds
Clouds painted across the sky's canvas with tears that evaporated into memorials that we rain dance to in triumph
Hearts pounding like war drums
This a war forged in colonial scars that shape shifted into alcoholic blissfulness
The rez is drowning in whiskey tears and for some reason they think change is best served from the belly of a slot machine

Isaac J Torres

As if any amount of currency can cure the systemic plague of assimilation
injected into a lineage of tattered nations
A forgotten people
Force fed Christianity while Jesus wept to symphonies of their slaughter
I bare the facial features of my people yet they refuse to acknowledge me
Fast forward to now
Watch as they cheer to the buffoonery of mascots
masquerading like misrepresentation
A sea of head dresses pressed against hooded linens
that sting our souls like hooded sheets
Or statistics that read like the definition of poverty stricken
We were PTSD before it ever became a diagnosis
Listen to our song with a heart so full of love
that it is one beat from bursting with empathy
I am a prototype
A savage no longer
Foggy eyed while lip-syncing songs that celebrate
the atrocities of my ancestors demise
Hyphenated
Disconnected
Searching for my roots in a forest of neo-democracy
Swimming against the current
Reaching for the sun
Dancing across the midnight sky
Flowing in the mountains
A wind song echoing eternally
Guided by a mother's love
A father's sacrifice
Dreaming of infinity

Isaac J Torres: Whether its skeletons, struggle, taboo, politics, or the beautiful chaos that is life, Ike Torres attacks all angles of the human narrative by incorporating the arts of spoken word, comedy, theatre, monologue, music, and improvisation to provide the audience with an experience that will leave them laughing, crying, and severely entertained.

The World Over

Let's change the world before the fire
Of injustice burn the little buds growing up
Let's redefine humanity all over again
Before all this tension wipes out the human race

Let's redefine the power of people's unity
This can form a strong circle around the globe
Let's leave behind alienation and poverty
And the path created by tyrants

Let's redefine ownership with every human being in mind
So we can divide the big luxury houses sitting empty
Waiting for the homeless to move in
And make use of those lonely houses with no tenants

Mahnaz Badihian is a poet, painter and translator whose work has been published into several languages worldwide, including Persian, Kurdish, French, Turkish, Spanish and Malayalam. Her work has appeared in many literary magazines including *exiled ink!* In the United Kingdom, International poetry magazine and in Marin Poetry Center Anthology amongst others. She attended the Iowa Writer's workshop with a focus on international poetry while practicing as a dentist in Iowa City. She won an award for a selection of her poetry (XIV Premio Letterario Internazionale Trofeo Penna d'Autore, Tornio) translated into Italian by Cristina Contili and Pirooz Ebrahimi. Currently, she resides in Northern California where she runs an online multilingual literary magazine, MahMag.org in an effort to bring the poetry of the world together. She presented a paper on erotic literature by Iranian women in the Diaspora at the American Comparative Literature Association's 2008 annual conference. Mahnaz was a resident Artis in Camac France in 2011. In the summer of 2013, she participated in the World Festival of Poetry to join poets from around the world in Peru and Bolivia. She received her MFA in poetry from Pacific University. She is currently working on a collection called "Recycled Woman."

Mahnaz Badihian

The Embarcadero is a Place Where Lawyers Live

Today, lawyers live on the Embarcadero
but they didn't used to.

In Spanish "Embarcadero" means commercial port
and in San Francisco in 1971
it was where the world's commercial armada
loaded and unloaded its gross national product

But no more,

Today the ships are gone
the docks are fit for the gentry
and lawyers live on the Embarcadero.

But once upon-a-time
in the cool early mist and smell of wooden planks soaked in salt air
the "little cat's feet" caressed the skin of dockworkers.
to the sounds of seabirds echoing off steel-hulled freighters:
a place where longshoremen worked in warehouses and cargo holds
for high wages, health plan, overtime, and a pension.

But they had to fight for it ...

General Strike!
In 1934 "The City" stopped working when longshoremen struck
– merchants shuttered shops
– service workers stopped serving
– transportation unions shut off their motors
– and nobody worked,

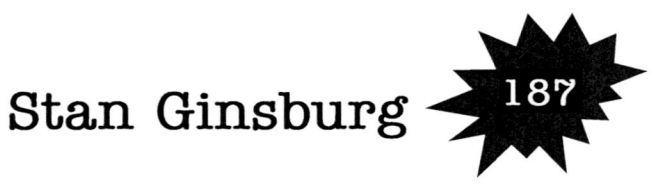

Stan Ginsburg

When Pinkertons and National Guard shot down a few strikers
working people paraded down Market Street
carrying caskets of slaughtered union brothers
while ordinary citizens lined sidewalks in solidarity

But that was yesterday:
today lawyers live on the Embarcadero.

Back then, some said Eddie Machen was the toughest guy on the docks:
a ranked heavyweight who fought Patterson, Frazier, Liston
and later slung coffee sacks for a living,
while others said the toughest guy was Harry Bridges:
the legendary labor hero who built a union that nobody fucked with ...

... until the containers came.

Still the Union fought back,
shutting down ports on both coasts
and bosses had to truck cargo into the US
from ports in Esenada and Vancouver
until Nixon's Taft Hartley decree ended the strike

But there was more ...

One day, opposite the "port" side of Embarcadero Street on the dry side,
the developers' construction crews began work on a "mixed-use complex."

Few took notice as the din of their jackhammers, bulldozers, and nail guns
mingled across the street from dockworkers and teamsters,
and their forklifts, cranes and big rigs
all dwarfed by cargo ships
the biggest machines in the neighborhood.

In this world of heavy equipment mountain moving diesel fumes,
the guys on the dock side of Embarcadero didn't yet care
that the guys across the street were digging a big hole
where a piece of the city would soon be buried
and lawyers would one-day park their cars.

(The Embarcadero was supposed to be a place
for guys with longshoreman's hooks dangling from back pockets,
who needed gloves to work
and could sling sacks of coffee
and single-handedly roll 50-gallon oil drums onto a pallet
... all day long.)

For a while
the solid growl of the construction crews
amplified the steady rumble of longshoremen and Teamsters:
all big guys
with big hands
doing big work.

But this too passed.

Today, as dawn melts the misty cool
sleepy Embarcadero sidewalks wake
to babies and happy pups being jogged
along this gentrified piece of the civic jigsaw
where "little cable cars"
marry Chinatown, Fisherman's Wharf, and North Beach,
to "The Embarcadero"
whose port, piers and warehouses
have shrunk to chic Gallerias,
pushing elegance, glamour, and proud coffee table books
capturing with ghostly photo pride
       an "Historic" San Francisco.

Stan Ginsburg is an L.A. based writer and retired high school English teacher, who worked in S.F. as a longshoreman decades ago. Another poem about teaching for the LAUSD, titled "Wounded Angels," was recently published in the *Coiled Serpent* poetry anthology.

190

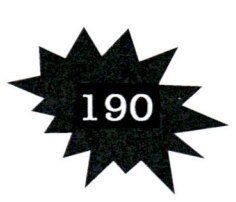

The First and
The Last
of Everything

The first cry of man in the first light

The first firefly flickering at night

The first song of love and forty cries of despair

The first voyage of Vikings westward

The first sighting of the New World
  from the crow's nest of a Spanish galleon

The first Pale Face meeting the first Native American

The first Dutch trader in Mannahatta

The first settler on the first frontier

The first Home Sweet Home so dear

The first wagon train westward

The first sighting of the Pacific by Lewis & Clark

The first cry of "Mark, twain!" on the Mississippi

The first desegregation by Huck & Jim on a raft at night

The first buffalo-head nickel and the last buffalo

The first barbed-wire fence and the last of the open range

The last cowboy on the last frontier

Lawrence Ferlinghetti

The first skyscraper in America

The first home run hit at Yankee Stadium

The first ballpark hotdog with mustard

The last War To End All Wars

The last Wobbly and the last Catholic Anarchist

The last living member of the Abraham Lincoln Brigade

The last bohemian in a beret

The last homespun politician and the first stolen election

The first plane to hit the first Twin Tower

The birth of a vast national paranoia

The first President to become an international criminal
      for crimes against humanity
           making America a terrorist state

The dark dawn of American corporate fascism

The next-to-last free speech radio

The next-to-last independent newspaper raising hell

The next-to-last independent bookstore with a mind of its own

The next-to-last lefty looking for Obama Nirvana

The first fine day of a White House Occupation

to set forth upon this continent a new nation!*

This poem in a slightly-different form was published in the Nation Magazine in 2015. The last line of the poem is a quote from Lincoln's Gettysburg Address.

THE LAST LORD'S PRAYER

Our father whose art's in heaven
Hollow be thy name
Unless things change
Thy kingdom come and gone
Thy will will be undone
On earth as it isn't heaven
Give us this day our daily bread
At least three times a day
And lead us not into temptation
Too often on weekdays
But deliver us from evil
Whose presence remains unexplained
In thy kingdom of power and glory
Oh man!

Lawrence Ferlinghetti is a prominent voice of the wide-open poetry movement that began in the 1950s, Lawrence Ferlinghetti has written poetry, translation, fiction, theater, art criticism, film narration, and essays. Often concerned with politics and social issues, Ferlinghetti's poetry countered the literary elite's definition of art and the artist's role in the world. Though imbued with the commonplace, his poetry cannot be simply described as polemic or personal protest, for it stands on his craftsmanship, thematics, and grounding in tradition. Ferlinghetti's *A Coney Island of the Mind* continues to be the most popular poetry book in the U.S. It has been translated into nine languages, and there are nearly 1,000,000 copies in print. A 50th anniversary edition was published by New Directions in 2008. The author of poetry, plays, fiction, art criticism, and essays, he has a dozen books currently in print in the U.S., and his work has been translated in many countries and in many languages. His most recent poetry books are *Americus Book I* (2004), *Poetry As Insurgent Art* (2007), and *Time of Useful Conscsiouness* (2012) all published by New Directions. His most recent work of poetry is the chapbook *Blasts Cries Laughter* (2014).

Lawrence Ferlinghetti

194

Wakin' & Walkin':
The Mournin' After

disabled nation:
howling long
for your bluescentric/
bluescestral home

enslaver & enslaved – ripening in your grave--
twist, shout & rise as lynchee, royalty & knave:

loom like a people-width pall
fossils ntu gems
ntu hollas
ntu hymns

I
poets breathe *All Blues*--mile after mile of Miles--ntu chilled "hoarse air"

II
soulo-*Walkin'* brother "ain't doin' so good" in quest to heal short-changed hood

III
here go Walt, Langston, Jimmy. Maya & Toni. Mojohn & Afrohorn

IV
ugly glory & sweet defeat: make USA grate again? howl long

V
a crippled climate cripples villages fermenting in the gods' *blues-people*

VI
howl long for bluescestral home

Eugene B. Redmond

AN EPISTOLARY JOURNAL (KWANSABA-STYLE)
RE: CENTENNIAL OF JOHN OLIVER KILLENS (1916-1987): BIG DADDY OF BLACK WRITING & BLACK WRITERS CONFERENCES

I
Shining for eager scribes at CUNY Brooklyn's
Black Writers Conference-'86, Margaret & Maya
called you "John O"--while the *caged
bird* crashed at your Crown Heights castle.
Today, I still wear your words like
ankhs, proudly shape-shiftin' them ntu agbadas
that warm me on cold white nights.

II
As a mid-50's to mid-80's
mid-husband of "long-distance runners" (your
'73 *Black Scholar* essay notes Troupe &
me), you "distance"-wrote & noveled Black
life matters: *Youngblood*-'54/*Thunder*-'64/*Cotillion*-
'71. But despite three-for-three "nominations,"
Pulitzer would award no prizes those years.

III: 1986: What you said about Margaret Walker:

"'For My People'--the
greatest poem in the Anglo-
Saxon Language!" Period.

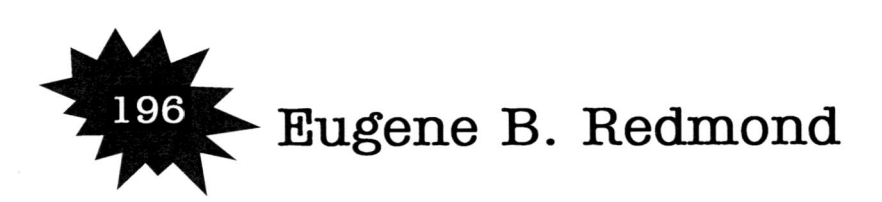

Eugene B. Redmond

IV
Georgia & The Great Migration had you
on their minds a century ago. Fisk
too. And Howard. Columbia. Soular-Sippi origins
of Harlem Writers Guild & Medgar Evers
College. DuBois. Robeson. Hueman strains of Zora-
Richard-Billie's trio. Up above heads, "John
O," long-distance "Thunder" hails "Stormy Weather."

Spring 2016

Eugene B. Redmond is a poet, educator, scholar and arts activist. He is the longest serving Poet Laureate in the United States, serving East St. Louis since 1977. His books include *Drum Voices*, a seminal study of modern African American poetry; *Eye in the Ceiling: Selected Poems*, recipient of the American Book Award, and *Arkansippi Memwars: Poems, Prose, and Chants 1962-2012*. Redmond is the inspiration and guiding light for the Eugene B. Redmond Writers Club, celebrating its thirtieth year of mentoring writers and producing culturally enriching programming.

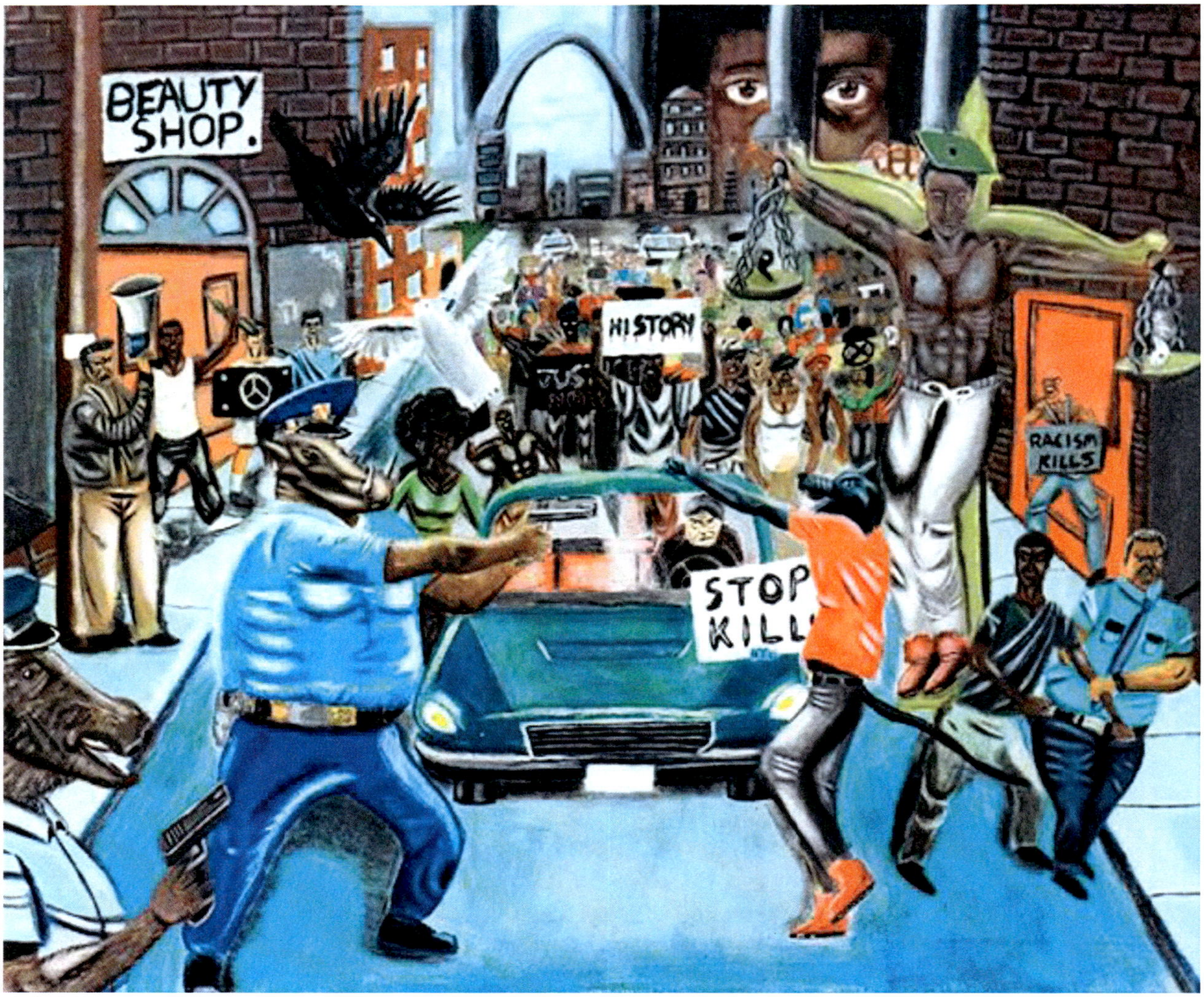
BEAUTY SHOP.
HISTORY
STOP
KILL
RACISM KILLS

FOR THE DEEDS OF MEN LIVE ON
with a nod to William Shakespeare

Friends, comrades, fellow Americans
      lend me your ears.

We have come here to bury fascism
      not to praise it
      not to negotiate with it
      not to give it a chance
      but to put it in its rightful grave.

The evil that men do lives after them.

Though memories be short in the computer age
      we still remember that
      we've been down this road before
      and pledged to ourselves,
      never again.

We do not come here to fear the future
      but to confront it – head on
      and shape it – with our own hands
      in the names of Democracy
      and Justice for All,
      not just the wealthy.

For the deeds of men live on and we remember
      the generations of lies and betrayal,
      the wars for profits
      to line the pockets
      of the greedy few.

Mark Lipman

While Wall Street thugs
      wrecked our economy
      to the sound of applause
      from both sides of the aisle.

Making backroom deals
      with handshakes and smiles
      all the while leaving
      We, the People
      hanging out to dry.

So, we have come here today,
      to remind you precisely what the words
      "of," "by" and "for" really mean.

And just in case you cannot read between these lines
      allow me to define what we have come here to say,

"Enough!"

Our future is not for sale.

Our rights, as human beings include things like:

Healthcare and retirement,
a clean environment, good education
and a home to live in
– guaranteed regardless of one's stature
– just like any other responsible country on this planet
simply for the fact of being – a human being.

For the deeds of men live on
      and it's about time
      that we started to live up
      to our true potential.

So, we have come here today to bury fascism.

If you think it's safe to attack
      someone who's Black, or Latino, Asian, Muslim
      gay, female, poor, or simply different
      just because they're weaker than you ...
      then you've got another thing coming.

Remember that the people are united
      if you mess with any of us
      you mess with all of us.

Now, we did not come here
      to spoil your breakfast
      but to make it manifest
      that our destiny is our own
      and woe to those who do not know
      the government is there to serve the people.

So sit back, relax, enjoy your day, do not be forlorn
      for what you see here – this, well this,
      this is simply the calm before the storm.

AMIRI BARAKA

Amiri Baraka told me last night
  that when they're dishing out the punishment
  how much you receive
  will match exactly to
  what you're willing to take.

If they kick you in the ass three times
  and you don't say a word
  you can be sure that number four
  is waiting right around the corner.

When you finally stand up
  and fight back
  and make a ruckus
  that is when they'll take you serious.

When they want to
  silence your words
  you had better speak louder.

Just like Robeson did
  when they stole his passport
  setting up a stage
  on the U.S. side of the border
  while thousands of Canadians
  lined up on the other side
  to hear what he had to say.

Mark Lipman

If they won't print your words
   start your own publishing house.

If they won't let you on stage
   start your own theater.

If what you've got to say
   is making them that uncomfortable
   then you must be on the right track.

When you're lying on your back
   chained to the floor
   at the bottom of the boat
   wondering how you got there
   alone in the darkness
   and they've taken your
   Oom boom ba boom
   away from you …

When they've taken your
   Oom boom ba boom
   away from you
   you know you're in
   some serious shit.

It may take hundreds of years
   and generations
   for you to get it back
   but you owe it to
   that river of bones
   lying at the bottom of the Atlantic
   to keep the fight alive.

Injustice never goes away
   the struggle is always with us
   the only question is,

What are you going to do
                about it?

Mark Lipman, founder of VAGABOND; recipient of the 2015 Joe Hill Labor Poetry Award; winner of the 2016 International Latino Book Award for *The Border Crossed Us (an anthology to end apartheid)*; a writer, poet, multi-media artist and activist, is the author of seven books, most recently, *Imposing Democracy; Poetry for the Masses;* and *Global Economic Amnesty.* Co-founder of the Berkeley Stop the War Coalition (USA), Agir Contre la Guerre (France) and Occupy Los Angeles, he has been an outspoken critic of war and occupation since 2001. Mark uses poetry to connect communities to the greater social issues that affect all of our lives, while building consciousness through the spoken word. Currently, he is a member of POWER (People Organized for Westside Renewal), the IWW (Industrial Workers of the World), Occupy Venice, the Revolutionary Poets Brigade and 100 Thousand Poets for Change.

BE THIS GUY

204

Index of Artwork

9 / La Charge, by Artactqc.com
14 / Standing Rock Buffalo, No DAPL
20 / Crying Lady Liberty, by Michael Lynch
27 / The New Age of Slavery, by Patrick Capmbell
37 / Resistance becomes Duty, Thomas Jefferson
50 / Detroit Industry Mural (detail), by Diego Rivera
66 / My Unhappy Place, by Alex Scheafer
80 / I Can't Breathe, by Audrey McNamara
90 / Police Brutality, by Neal Fox
96 / Arresting Liberty, Democracy Spring, Associated Press
100 / Rising Tide, unknown artist
112 / Nuthin' to See Here, Keep on Movin'!, by Vincent Valdez
119 / Ferguson Riot Police #1, Associated Press
134 / On the Wrong Side of Capitalism, unknown photographer
147 / BLM Protest Phoenix, Associated Press
156 / If the Workers Take a Notion, Joe Hill
166 / Mine Workers, unknown artist
172 / Political Clown Circus, by Steven LaPierre
190 / I Stand with Standing Rock, No DAPL
194 / Must Turn Left, unknown photographer
198 / Untitled #1, by David Pulphus
204 / Be this Guy, August Landmesser

VAGABOND

www.vagabondbooks.net